How to Raise and Train a

MINIATURE SCHNAUZER

By

Leda B. Martin and Sara M. Barbaresi

Distributed in the U.S.A. by T.F.H. Publications, Inc., 211 West Sylvania Avenue, P.O. Box 27, Neptune City, N.J. 07753; in England by T.F.H. (Gt. Britain) Ltd., 13 Nutley Lane, Reigate, Surrey; in Canada to the book store and library trade by Clarke, Irwin & Company, Clarwin House, 791 St. Clair Avenue West, Toronto 10, Ontario; in Canada to the pet trade by Rolf C. Hagen Ltd., 3225 Sartelon Street, Montreal 382, Quebec; in Southeast Asia by Y.W. Ong, 9 Lorong 36 Geylang, Singapore 14; in Australia and the south Pacific by Pet Imports Pty. Ltd., P.O. Box 149, Brookvale 2100, N.S.W., Australia. Published by T.F.H. Publications, Inc. Ltd., The British Crown Colony of Hong Kong.

ACKNOWLEDGMENTS

Pictures were taken by Three Lions, Inc., with the cooperation of Ledahof Kennels, New Brunswick, New Jersey.

ISBN 0-87666-338-2

Library of Congress Catalog Card No. 58-7601
Manufactured in the United States of America

Contents

A handsome champion Miniature Schnauzer poses in front of some his ribbons and trophies.

1. Schnauzer Standards

The Schnauzer comes in three varieties: Giant, Standard and Miniature, the smallest and most popular. All are natives of Germany, where the breed was developed to be guardian of the house and farm, rat-killer and companion.

The Miniature Schnauzer is classified as a Terrier in the United States, although it is descended from Pudel and Pinscher stock, and is not closely related to the English members of the Terrier group, such as the Airedale, Fox Terrier and Scottie. However, the Schnauzer's alert and lively temperament is typical of the Terrier. He is of sturdy but compact build, under fourteen inches in height and about fifteen pounds or less in weight, small enough for apartment dwelling but rugged enough to lead an outdoor country life.

Although a medium salt and pepper is the color most frequently seen, the Schnauzer may range from silver to solid black. His whiskers, beard and bushy eyebrows are distinctive features. The Schnauzer should have a heavy coat on the legs, and a shorter and harsher body coat. A professional stripping twice a year, which you can learn to do yourself, will keep him looking tidy.

HISTORY OF THE BREED

The original Schnauzer was of Standard size, a farm dog not used for digging out vermin as were the smaller English terriers. However, crosses of the Standard with smaller working dogs, or with the small short-faced black Affenpinscher or "monkey terrier," resulted in a smaller variety, originally called the Dwarf *(Zwergschnauzer)* and then the Miniature Schnauzer. The name Schnauzer comes fom the whiskered muzzle or snout. All this breeding took place before 1900, and the breed has been kept pure since then. Various registries have kept records for more than 60 years in Germany, and the breed was already known throughout Europe by the beginning of the 20th century.

It was not until 1923 that the first Miniature Schnauzers came to this country, and the first American-breds were born several years later. They first competed in the same classes with Standard Schnauzers in the shows, and then, until American Kennel Club recognition in 1926, in the Miscellaneous Class. A combined Schnauzer Club was the sponsor and ruling organization for several years, and a separate American Miniature Schnauzer Club was formed in 1933. The present secretary is Mrs. W. F. Ackerman, 10 Catalpa Road, Morristown, New Jersey. Write to her or to the American Kennel Club, 221 Fourth Ave., New York 3, New York, for information concerning breeders in your vicinity or club activities.

The standard by which the Miniature Schnauzer is judged, recently adopted by the A.M.S.C. and approved by the A.K.C., follows.

DESCRIPTION AND STANDARD OF POINTS

GENERAL APPEARANCE: The Miniature Schnauzer is a robust, active dog of terrier type, resembling his larger cousin, the Standard Schnauzer, in general appearance, and of an alert, active disposition. He is sturdily built, nearly square in proportion of body length to height, with plenty of bone, and without any suggestion of toyishness.

HEAD: Strong and rectangular, its width diminishing slightly from ears to eyes, and again to the tip of the nose. The forehead is unwrinkled. The top skull is flat and fairly long. The foreface is parallel to the top skull, with a slight stop; and it is at least as long as the top skull. The muzzle is strong in proportion to the skull; it ends in a moderately blunt manner, with thick whiskers which accentuate the rectangular shape of the head.

TEETH: The teeth meet in a scissors bite. That is, the upper front teeth overlap the lower front teeth in such a manner that the inner surface of the upper incisors barely touches the outer surface of the lower incisors when the mouth is closed.

EYES: Small, dark brown and deep-set. They are oval in appearance and keen in expression.

EARS: When cropped the ears are identical in shape and length, with pointed tips. They are in balance with the head and not exaggerated in length. They are set high on the skull and carried perpendicularly at the inner edges, with as little bell as possible along the outer edges. When uncropped the ears are small and v-shaped, folding close to the skull.

NECK: Strong and well arched, blending into the shoulders, and with the skin fitting tightly at the throat.

BODY: Short and deep, with the brisket extending at least to the elbows. Ribs are well sprung and deep, extending well back to a short loin. The underbody does not present a tucked-up appearance at the flank. The topline is straight; it declines slightly from the withers to the base of the tail. The overall length from chest to stern bone equals the height at the withers.

FOREQUARTERS: The forequarters have flat, somewhat sloping shoulders and high withers. Forelegs are straight and parallel when viewed from all sides. They have strong pasterns and good bone. They are separated

A Miniature Schnauzer is an excellent pet for a child, particularly if the two grow up together. This boy and dog are obviously good friends already.

by a fairly deep brisket which precludes a pinched front. The elbows are close, and the ribs spread gradually from the first rib so as to allow space for the elbows to move close to the body.

HINDQUARTERS: The hindquarters have strong-muscled, slanting thighs; they are well bent at the stifles and straight from hock to so-called heel. There is sufficient angulation so that, in stance, the hocks extend beyond the tail. The hindquarters never appear overbuilt or higher than the shoulders.

FEET: Short and round (cat-feet) with thick, black pads. The toes are arched and compact.

The Miniature Schnauzer's distinctive eyebrows and whiskers show to good advantage here.

ACTION: The trot is the gait at which movement is judged. The dog must gait in a straight line. Coming on, the forelegs are parallel, with the elbows close to the body. The feet turn neither inward nor outward. Going away, the hind legs are parallel from the hocks down, and travel wide. Viewed from the side, the forelegs have a good reach, while the hind legs have a strong drive with good pick-up of hocks.

TAIL: Set high and carried erect. It is docked only long enough to be clearly visible over the top line of the body when the dog is in proper length of coat.

COAT: Double, with a hard, wiry outer coat and a close under coat. The body coat should be plucked. When in show condition, the proper length is not less than three-quarters of an inch except on neck, ears and skull. Furnishings are fairly thick but not silky.

SIZE: From 12 to 14 inches. Ideal size 13½ inches. *See Disqualifications.*

COLOR: The recognized colors are salt and pepper, black and silver, and solid black. The typical color is salt and pepper in shades of gray; tan shading is permissible. The salt and pepper mixture fades out to light gray or silver white in the eyebrows, whiskers, cheeks, under throat, across chest, under tail, leg furnishings, under body, and inside legs. The light under-body hair is not to rise higher on the sides of the body than the front elbows.

The black and silvers follow the same pattern as the salt and peppers. The entire salt and pepper section must be black.

Children can care for and train their own dogs, and learn responsibility in the process. This youngster is training his dog to sit.

Black is the only solid color allowed. It must be a true black with no gray hairs and no brown tinge except where the whiskers may have become discolored. A small white spot on the chest is permitted.

FAULTS

TYPE: Toyishness, raciness, or coarseness.

STRUCTURE: Head coarse and cheeky. Chest too broad or shallow in brisket. Tail set low. Sway or roach back. Bowed or cowhocked hindquarters. Loose elbows.

ACTION: Sidegaiting. Paddling in front, or high hackney knee action. Weak hind action.

COAT: Too soft or too smooth and slick in appearance.

TEMPERAMENT: Shyness or viciousness.

BITE: Undershot or overshot jaw. Level bite.

EYES: Light and/or large and prominent in appearance.

DISQUALIFICATIONS

Dogs or bitches under 12 inches or over 14 inches.
Color solid white or white patches on the body.

2. Buying Your Miniature Schnauzer

Once you have decided that you want a Schnauzer, the next thing to do is to go about getting him or her. Perhaps you chose the breed because a neighbor's dog had puppies and your children talked you into it. If the pups are for sale, your task is an easy one. But it is more likely that you just decided that the Schnauzer is the dog for you, and now you have to find the right one.

First, make up your mind what you want: male or female, adult or puppy, show dog or "just a pet." There is no greater use for a dog than being "just" a beloved pet and companion, but the dog which has profitable show and breeding possibilities is worth more to the seller.

PET OR SHOW DOG?

The puppy with a slight flaw in his ear carriage or quantity of coat will make just as good a companion and guardian, but his more perfect littermate will cost more.

That is why there is often a difference in price between puppies which look—to you, anyway—identical. If you think you may want to show your dog or raise a litter of puppies for the fun of it later on, by all means buy the best you can afford. You will save expense and disappointment later on. However, if the puppy is *strictly* a pet for the children, or companion for you, you can afford to look for a bargain. The pup which is not show material; the older pup, for which there is often less demand; or the grown dog, not up to being used for breeding, are occasionally available and are opportunities to save money. Remember that these are the only real bargains in buying a dog. It takes good food and care—and plenty of both—to raise a healthy, vigorous puppy.

The price you pay for your dog is little compared to the love and devotion he will return over the many years he'll be with you. With good care and affection your pup should live to a ripe old age; through modern veterinary science and nutrition, dogs are better cared for and living longer. Their average life expectancy is now eight or nine years, and dogs in their teens are not uncommon.

This Schnauzer is ready to start off for a new home with his young owner. Many happy times are ahead.

MALE OR FEMALE?

If you should intend breeding your dog in the future, by all means buy a female. You can find a suitable mate without difficulty when the time comes, and have the pleasure of raising a litter of pups—there is nothing cuter than a fat, playful puppy. If you don't want to raise puppies, your female can be spayed, and will remain a healthy, lively pet. The female is smaller than the male and generally quieter. She has less tendency to roam in search of romance, but a properly trained male can be a charming pet, and has a certain difference in temperament that is appealing to many people. Male vs. female is chiefly a matter of personal choice.

Above: Training should begin as soon as you get your dog. Be firm if you want him to stay off the furniture.

Below: Your Schnauzer will not object to being bathed if you get him used to it early.

ADULT OR PUP?

Whether to buy a grown dog or a small puppy is another question. It is undeniably fun to watch your dog grow all the way from a baby, sprawling and playful, to a mature, dignified dog. If you don't have the time to spend on the more frequent meals, housebreaking, and other training a puppy needs in order to become a dog you can be proud of, then choose an older, partly trained pup or a grown dog. If you want a show dog, remember that no one, not even an expert, can predict with 100% accuracy what a small puppy will be when he grows up. Someone familiar with dogs may be right *most* of the time, but six months is the earliest age for the would-be exhibitor to pick a prospect and know that his future is relatively safe.

The newborn Schnauzer puppy already shows the beginnings of pepper-and-salt marking. Tiny puppies must be handled very gently.

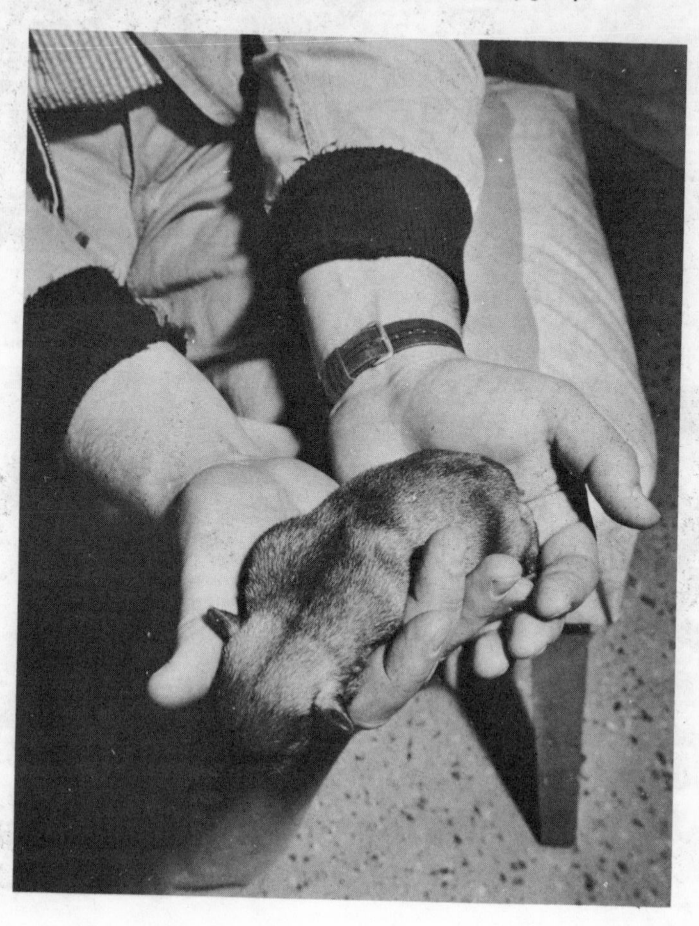

At two weeks the puppy's eyes are just about to open. He will not be ready to leave home for another month.

If you have a small child it is best to get a puppy big enough to protect himself, one not less than four or five months old. Older children will enjoy playing with and helping to take care of a baby pup, but at less than four months a puppy wants to do little but eat and sleep, and he must be protected from teasing and overtiring. You cannot expect a very young child to understand that a puppy is a fragile living being; to the youngster he is a toy like a stuffed dog.

WHERE TO BUY

You can choose among several places to buy your dog. One is a kennel which breeds show dogs as a business and has extra pups for sale as pets.

Above: Your dog will need a little time to get used to his new surroundings.

Below: Some of these Miniature Schnauzer puppies may become show dogs; all of them will make handsome pets.

Another is the one-dog owner who wants to sell the puppies from an occasional litter and thus pay his expenses. Pet shops usually buy puppies from overstocked kennels or part-time hobbyists for re-sale, and you can generally buy a puppy there at a reasonable price. To find any of these, watch the pet column of your local newspaper or look in the classified section of your phone book. If you or your friends go driving out in the countryside, be on the lookout for a sign announcing purebred puppies for sale.

Whichever source you try, you can usually tell in a very short time whether the puppies will make healthy and happy pets. If they are clean, fat and lively, they are probably in good health. At the breeder's you will have the advantage of seeing the puppies' mother and perhaps the father and other relatives. Remember that the mother, having just raised a demanding family, won't be looking her best, but if she is sturdy, friendly and well-mannered, her puppies should be, too. If you feel that something is lacking in the care or condition of the dogs, it is better to look elsewhere than to buy hastily and regret it afterward.

You may be impatient to bring home your new dog, but a few days will make little difference in his life with you. Often it is a good idea to choose a puppy and put a deposit on him, but wait to take him home until you have prepared for the new arrival. For instance, it is better for the Christmas puppy to be settled in his new home before the holidays, or else to wait until things have settled down afterward. You may want to wait until the puppy has completed his "shots," and if this is arranged in advance, it is generally agreeable.

If you cannot find the dog you want locally, write to the A.K.C. (page 6), for names of breeders near you, or to whom you can write for information. Puppies are often bought by mail from reputable breeders.

WHAT TO LOOK FOR IN A PUPPY

In choosing your puppy, assuming that it comes from healthy, well-bred parents, look for one that is friendly and outgoing. The biggest pup in the litter is apt to be somewhat overgrown or clumsy as a grown dog, while the appealing "poor little runt" may turn out to be a timid shadow—or have a Napoleon complex! If you want a show dog and have no experience in choosing the prospect, study the standard (page 6), but be advised by the breeder on the finer points of conformation. His prices will be in accord with the puppies' expected worth, and he will be honest with you because it is to his own advantage. He wants his good puppies placed in the public eye to reflect glory on him—and to attract future buyers.

You might also visit a dog show or two before buying your future entry. Watch the judges and talk to the exhibitors. Some will probably have young stock for sale. (For a list of coming dog shows, as well as other useful information on dog care, breeding, travel, and so forth, write to the Gaines Dog Research Center, 250 Park Avenue, New York 17, N. Y.)

The puppy should be square in general outline, of good size, solidly built and well-boned. His head should be in proportion to his size, rectangular, with scissors bite. Eyes should be dark and not too large, with little haw or inner eyelid showing in the corner. The forelegs should be straight, shoulder sloping and neck arched. The back should be level, tail set high, cut short and carried well. The coat should be hard and wiry; some of the puppy fuzz is usually trimmed by nine weeks, especially on the head. Ears will probably be cropped. They should be evenly shaped and set high. If uncropped, they should be small and folded forward.

Although the immature puppy will still be awkward, he should be able to step out briskly and put one foot in front of the other instead of meandering or crossing over in front of himself.

Now that you have paid your money and made your choice, you are ready to depart with puppy, papers and instructions. Make sure that you know his feeding routine, and take along some of the food. It is best to make any diet changes gradually so you do not upset his digestion. If the puppy is not fed before leaving he will ride comfortably on your lap where he can see out of the window. Take along a rag or newspapers for accidents.

PAPERS

When you buy your puppy you should receive his pedigree and registration certificate or application. These have nothing to do with licensing, which is a local regulation applying to purebred and mongrel alike. Find out the local ordinance in regard to age, etc., buy a license, and keep it on your dog whenever he is off your property.

Your dog's pedigree is a chart, for your information only, showing his ancestry. It is not part of his official papers. The registration certificate is the important part. If the dog was named and registered by his breeders you will want to complete the transfer and send it, with the fee of $1.00, to the American Kennel Club, 221 Fourth Ave., New York 3, N. Y. They will transfer the dog to your ownership in their records, and send a new certificate to you.

When you send in the transfer of ownership you may insert a name of your own choosing. Try to make it original; if other dogs have the same name, yours will have a numeral attached, like Hans XV. To avoid this, call him Hans von Schmidt, or any combination of your own names, or your street or town, or some other term which appeals to you. You may not use the kennel prefix in his pedigree without its owner's permission, as this is the breeder's trademark.

No matter what the puppy's registered name is, you will probably call him by a shorter "call name" he will learn to recognize.

Get the puppy's litter number from the breeder and include it on the form which is sent with a fee of $2.00 to the A.K.C.; the form must be filled out completely.

3. Care of the Schnauzer Puppy

BRINGING YOUR PUPPY HOME

When you bring your puppy home, remember that he is used to the peace and relative calm of a life of sleeping, eating and playing with his brothers and sisters. The trip away from all this is an adventure in itself, and so is adapting to a new home. So let him take it easy for awhile. Don't let the whole neighborhood pat and poke him at one time. Be particularly careful when children want to handle him, for they cannot understand the difference between the delicate living puppy and the toy dog they play with and maul. If the puppy is to grow up loving children and taking care of them, he must not get a bad first impression.

THE PUPPY'S BED

It is up to you to decide where the puppy will sleep. He should have his own place, and not be allowed to climb all over the furniture. He should sleep out of drafts, but not right next to the heat, which would make him too sensitive to the cold when he goes outside. If your youngster wants to share his bed with the puppy, that is all right, too, but the puppy must learn the difference between his bed and other furniture. Or he may sleep on a dog bed or in a box big enough to curl up in: a regulation dog crate or one made from a packing box, with bedding for comfort.

You have already decided where the puppy will sleep before you bring him home. Let him stay there, or in the corner he will soon learn is "his," most of the time, so that he will gain a sense of security from the familiar. Give the puppy a little milk with bread and kibble in it when he arrives, but don't worry if he isn't hungry at first. He will soon develop an appetite when he grows accustomed to his surroundings. The first night the puppy may cry a bit from lonesomeness, but if he has an old blanket or rug to curl up in he will be cozy. In winter a hot water bottle will help replace the warmth of his littermates, or the ticking of a clock may provide company.

Although the puppy will sleep indoors, he will benefit from an outdoor run of his own where he can be put to exercise and amuse himself. It does not have to be large for if he goes for walks and plays with you he will get enough exercise that way. He is much safer shut in his run than being left loose to follow a stray dog off your property and get into bad habits—if he isn't hit by a car first!

Of course if the dog is left in his run for any length of time he should have protection from the cold, rain or sun. A small but snug doghouse with a floor slightly off the ground will give him a place of his own. The run should be rectangular, and as big as you can conveniently make it, up to 15 x 30 feet, with strong wire fence which will keep your dog in and intruders out. The wire should be at least four feet high, as many dogs like to jump, and the gate should be fastened with a spring hook or hasp which is not likely to be unfastened by mischance.

FEEDING YOUR PUPPY

It is best to use the feeding schedule to which the puppy is accustomed, and stick to it except when you feel you can modify or improve it. You will probably want to feed the puppy on one of the commercially prepared dog foods as a base, flavoring it with table scraps and probably a little meat and fat when you have them. Remember that the dog food companies have prepared their food so that it is a balanced ration in itself, and, indeed, many dogs are raised on dog food alone. If you try to change this balance too much you are likely to upset your pet's digestion, and the dog will not be as well fed in the long run. Either kibble or meal is a good basic food, and the most economical way to feed your dog.

Milk is good for puppies and some grown dogs like it. Big bones are fine to chew on, especially for teething puppies, but small bones such as chicken, chop or fish bones are always dangerous; they may splinter or stick in the digestive tract. Table scraps such as meat, fat, or vegetables will furnish variety and vitamins, but fried or starchy foods such as potatoes and beans will not be of much food value. Adding a tablespoonful of fat (lard or drippings) to the daily food will keep your puppy's skin healthy and make his coat shine.

Remember that all dogs are individuals. The amount that will keep your dog in good health is right for him, not the "rule-book" amount. A feeding chart to give you some idea of what the average puppy will eat follows:

WEANING TO 3 MONTHS: *A.M.*—½ cup of Pablum and dog meal, mixed with warm water or milk. *Noon*—½ cup warm milk, with cereal, kibble, or biscuits. *P.M.*—2 tbs. chopped beef, 2 tbs. cereal or dog meal, vitamin and mineral supplements. *Bedtime*—½ cup warm milk, mixed with ¼ cup Pablum. Change gradually from Pablum to dog meal or kibble.

3-6 MONTHS: *A.M.*—½ cup meat with shredded wheat or cereal. *Noon*—1 cup milk, soft-boiled egg twice a week, or 1 cup cottage cheese. *P.M.*—½ cup meat with ½ cup dog meal; or kibble and water.

6 MONTHS-1 YEAR: *A.M.*—½ cup dog meal or cereal with cottage

At six weeks, puppies are just learning to eat. Four good meals a day will help them grow into healthy, sturdy dogs.

cheese or egg, and milk. Add vitamin and mineral supplements. *P.M.*–½ cup meat with ¾ cup kibble or meal, fat, table scraps.

OVER 1 YEAR: *A.M.*–Half of evening meal, or several dog biscuits. *P.M.*–¾ cup meat, ¾ cup dog food, mixed with meal, fat or table scraps.

HOUSEBREAKING YOUR PUPPY

As soon as you get your puppy you can begin to housebreak him but remember that you can't expect too much of him until he is five months old or so. A baby puppy just cannot control himself, so it is best to give him an opportunity to relieve himself before the need arises.

Don't let the puppy wander through the whole house; keep him in one or two rooms under your watchful eye. If he has been brought up on newspapers, keep a couple of pages handy on the floor. When he starts to whimper, puts his nose to the ground or runs around looking restless, take him to the paper before an "accident" occurs. After he has behaved, praise him and let him roam again. It is much better to teach him the right way than to punish him for misbehaving. Puppies are naturally clean and can be housebroken easily, given the chance. If a mistake should occur, and mistakes are bound to happen occasionally, wash the spot immediately with tepid water, followed by another rinse with water to which a few drops of vinegar have been added. A dog will return to the same place if there is any odor left, so it is important to remove all traces.

Remember that the puppy has to relieve himself after meals and whenever he wakes up, as well as sometimes in between. So take him outside as soon as he shows signs of restlessness indoors, and stay with him until he has performed. Then praise and pat him, and bring him back inside as a reward. Since he is used to taking care of himself outdoors, he will not want to misbehave in the house, and will soon let you know when he wants to go out.

You can combine indoor paper training and outdoor housebreaking by taking the puppy out when convenient and keeping newspaper available for use at other times. As the puppy grows older he will be able to control himself for longer periods. If he starts to misbehave in the house, without asking to go out first, scold him and take him out or to his paper. Punishment *after* the fact will accomplish nothing; the puppy cannot understand why he is being scolded unless it is immediate.

The older puppy or grown dog should be able to remain overnight in the house without needing to go out, unless he is ill. If your dog barks or acts restless, take him out once, but unless he relieves himself right away, take him back indoors and shut him in his quarters. No dog will soil his bed if he can avoid it, and your pet will learn to control himself overnight if he has to.

VETERINARY CARE

You will want your puppy to be protected against the most serious puppyhood diseases: distemper and infectious hepatitis. So your first action after getting him will be to take him to your veterinarian for his shots and a check-up, if he has not already received them. He may have had all or part of the immunization as early as two months of age, so check with the seller before you bring your puppy home.

You may give the puppy temporary serum which provides immunity for about two weeks, but nowadays permanent vaccine providing lifelong immunity can be given so early that the serum is seldom used, except as a precaution in outbreaks. The new vaccine is a combined prevention against distemper and hepatitis, and may be given in one or three shots (two weeks apart). Your veterinarian probably has a preferred type, so go along with him, as either method is protective in a very high percentage of cases.

There is now an effective anti-rabies vaccine, which you can give to your dog if there should be an outbreak of this disease in your neighborhood. It is not permanent, however, so unless local regulations demand it, there is little value in giving the vaccine in ordinary circumstances.

Take your puppy to his paper to relieve himself and praise him when he behaves. It is usually a good idea to combine indoor paper training and outdoor housebreaking.

WORMING

Your puppy has probably been wormed at least once, since puppies have a way of picking up worms, particularly in a kennel where they are exposed to other dogs. Find out when he was last wormed and the date, if any, for re-worming. Older dogs are usually able to throw off worms if they are in good condition when infected, but unless the puppy is given some help when he gets worms, he is likely to become seriously sick. New worm medicines containing the non-toxic but effective piperazines may be bought at your pet store or druggist's, and you can give them yourself. But remember to follow instructions carefully and do not worm the puppy unless you are sure he has worms.

If the puppy passes a long, string-like white worm in his stool or coughs one up, that is sufficient evidence, and you should proceed to worm him. Other indications are: general listlessness, a large belly, dull coat, mattery eye and coughing, but these could also be signs that your puppy is coming down with some disease. If you only *suspect* that he has worms, take him to your veterinarian for a check-up and stool examination before worming.

THE FEMALE PUPPY

If you want to spay your female you can have it done while she is still a puppy. Her first seasonal period will probably occur between eight and ten months, although it may be as early as six or delayed until she is a year old. She may be spayed before or after this, or you may breed her (at a later season) and still spay her afterward.

The first sign of the female's being in season is a thin red discharge, which will increase for about a week, when it changes color to a thin yellowish stain, lasting about another week. Simultaneously there is a swelling of the vulva, the dog's external sexual organ. The second week is the crucial period, when she could be bred if you want her to have puppies, but it is possible for the period to be shorter or longer, so it is best not to take unnecessary risks at any time. After a third week the swelling decreases and the period is over for about six months.

If you have an absolutely climb-proof and dig-proof run within your yard, it will be safe to leave her there, but otherwise the female in season should be shut indoors. Don't leave her out alone for even a minute; she should be exercised only on leash. If you want to prevent the neighborhood dogs from hanging around your doorstep, as they inevitably will as soon as they discover that your female is in season, take her some distance away from the house before you let her relieve herself. Take her in your car to a park or field for a chance to stretch her legs. After the three weeks are up you can let her out as before, with no worry that she can have puppies until the next season. But if you want to have her spayed, consult your veterinarian about the time and age at which he prefers to do it. With a young dog the operation is simple and after a night or two at the animal hospital she can be at home, wearing only a small bandage as a souvenir.

4. Caring for Your Adult Miniature Schnauzer

When your dog reaches his first birthday he is no longer a puppy, although he will not be fully mature and developed until he is two. For all intents and purposes, however, he may be considered full grown and adult now.

DIET

You may prefer to continue feeding your dog twice a day, although he can now eat all that he needs to be healthy at one meal a day. Usually it is best to feed that one meal, or the main meal, in the evening. Most dogs eat better this way, and digest their food better. If your dog skips an occasional meal, don't worry; after half an hour remove the food if he turns up his nose at it. Otherwise he will develop the habit of picking at his food, and food left out too long becomes stale or spoiled.

The best indication of the correct amount to feed your dog is his state of health. A fat dog is not a healthy one; just like a fat person, he has to strain his heart—and his whole body—to carry excess weight. If you cannot give your dog more exercise, cut down on his food, and remember that those dog biscuits fed as snacks or rewards count in the calories. If your dog is thin, increase the amount and add a little more fat. You can also add flavoring he likes to pep up his appetite. The average grown dog needs several cups of dog meal or a half-pound of canned food per day. Use your own judgment for YOUR dog.

CLEANLINESS AND GROOMING

The Miniature Schnauzer, with his clean ways, needs little in the way of grooming. From puppyhood he should be accustomed to frequent brushing, having his teeth checked, nails trimmed, and being handled.

If your pet does much running in woods and fields he will wear off his leg hair and whiskers which add so much to his appearance. If you wish to show him, this must be prevented, but your dog is better off anyway with only an occasional run off the leash when you are with him. A harsh, wiry coat is desirable and excess soft hair should be stripped out with a stripping knife or your fingers. The puppy coat is removed this way; cutting or clipping will make it soft and spoil the color effect, for the hairs are banded light and dark and produce the pepper and salt coloring. However, it is better to clip than to leave the coat long and unkempt. A coarse stripping knife is suitable for trimming and easy for an amateur to handle. (You can obtain an excellent chart showing how to trim your Schnauzer from the Durham-Enders Corporation, Mystic, Connecticut.)

Trim the hair so it lies quite flat, with long hair on the front legs and

You can use a stripping knife to remove your Miniature Schnauzer's excess soft hair. Strip the coat in the direction that it grows. For a neat appearance, the body hair should be kept quite short.

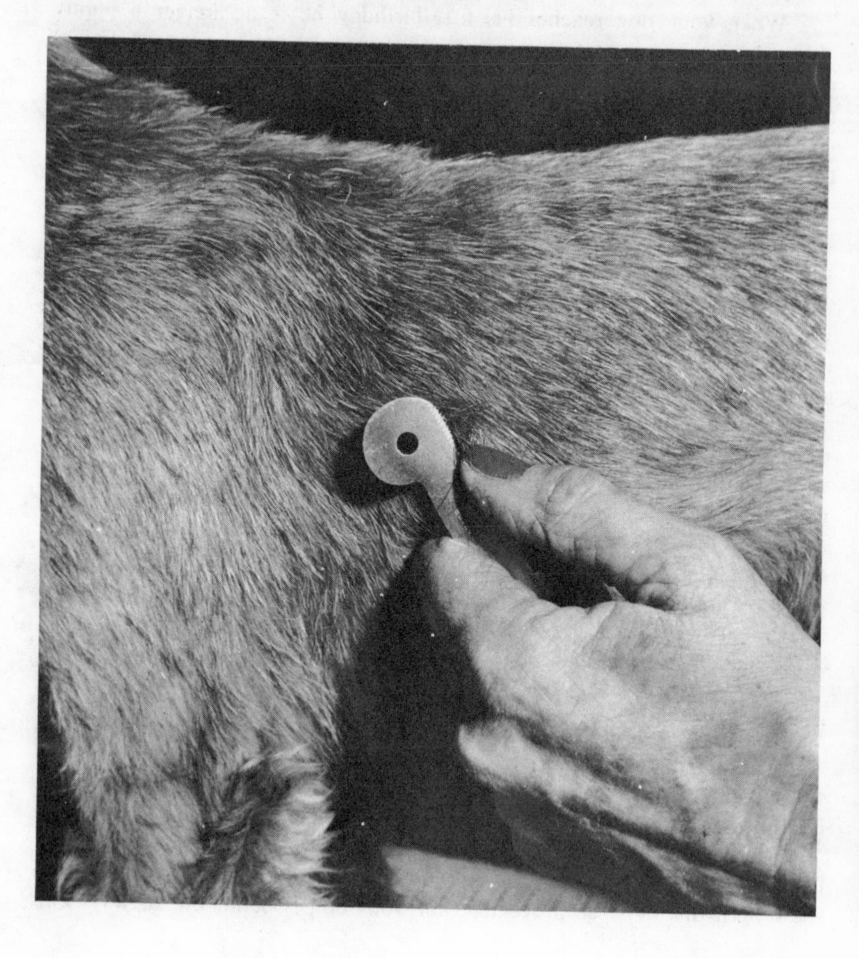

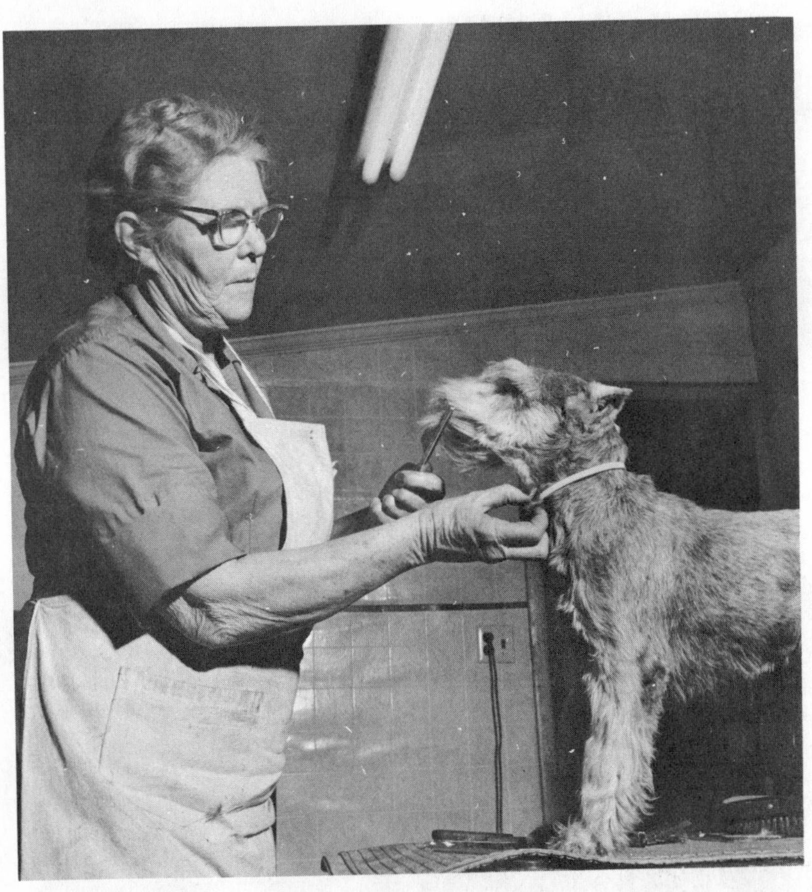

Comb your Schnauzer's whiskers to keep them neat and free from food and dirt. An occasional washing may be necessary.

below the hock, or heel, in back. After you have stripped out the body, proceed to trim head, legs and feet. Leave the hair long from eyebrows forward, but shape it to fit the head, and trim the rest of the head and ears close. Keep the dog's hindquarters neat for cleanliness and to make the body look more compact. Do not leave overlong hair on the belly and chest, although this adds to the body depth. Cut the hair between the toes short to make the foot neater, but around the edge trim it only to clear the ground. As the last part of the operation, even up, with scissors, the eyebrows, whiskers and leg furnishings to give the dog a tidy, sharp appearance.

The Schnauzer does not shed and if he is brushed and combed regularly he will always look well-groomed. If your dog becomes accustomed to brushing as a puppy, he will enjoy it. Teach him to jump onto a chest or large box

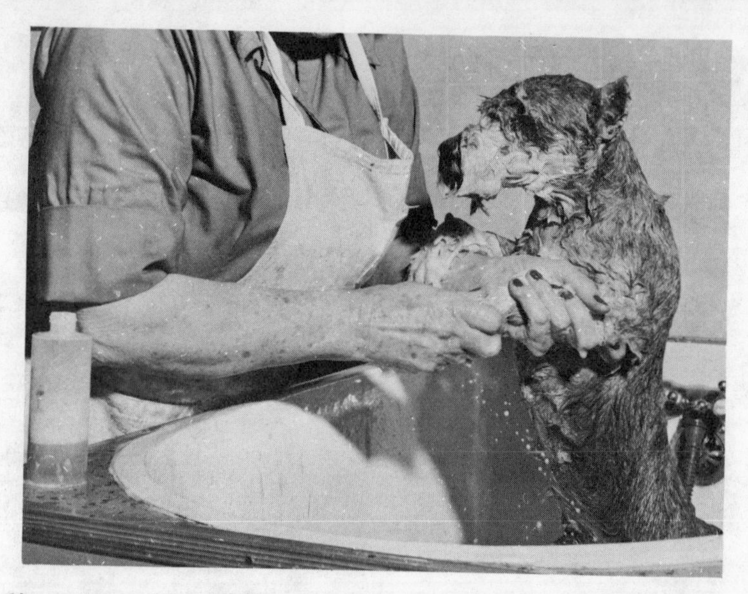

Above: Be careful not to get soap in your Schnauzer's eyes or ears when you bathe him.

Below: The whiskers and long hair on the feet and legs need special soaping if they are to be really clean.

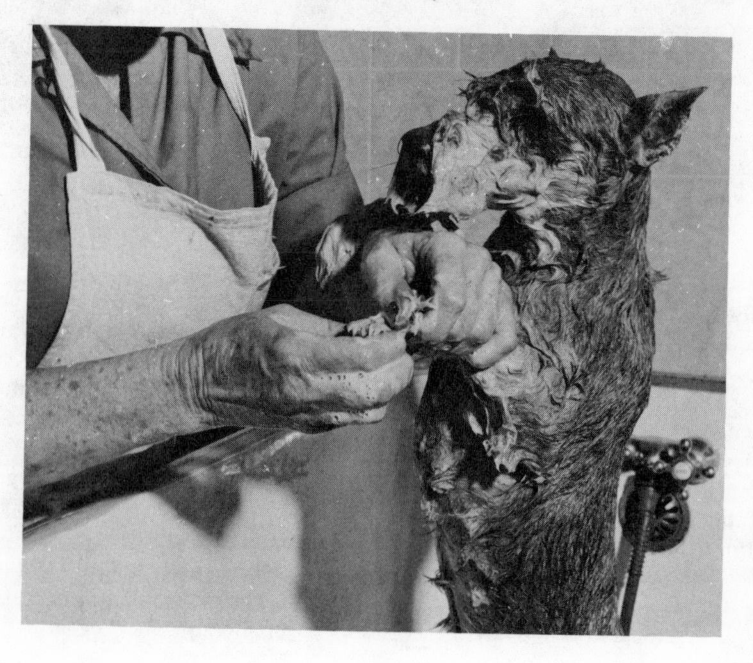

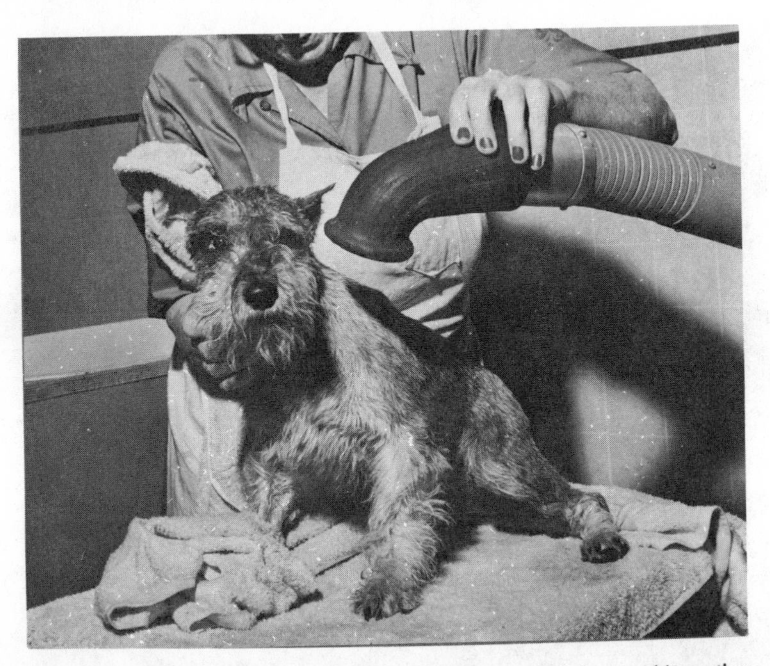

Above: Dry your Schnauzer thoroughly after his bath, especially in cold weather. Otherwise he may become chilled.

Below: Towel him briskly to remove most of the water, and then keep him in a warm place until he is completely dry.

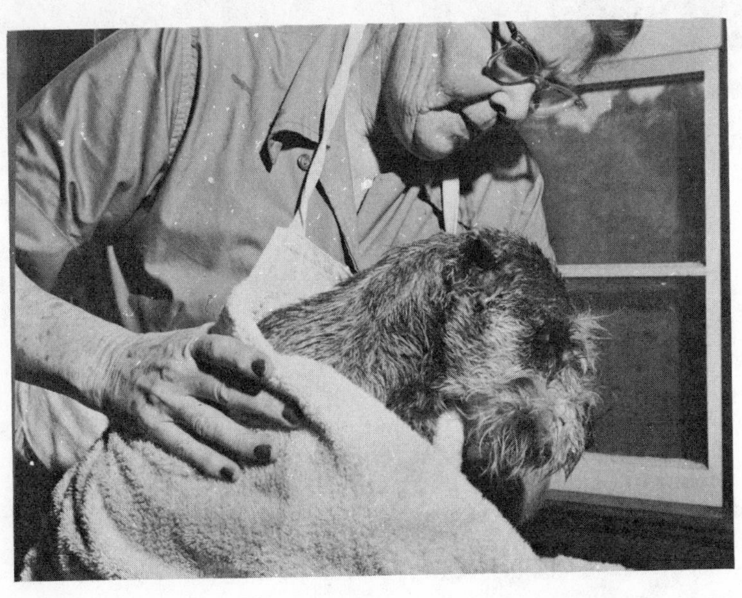

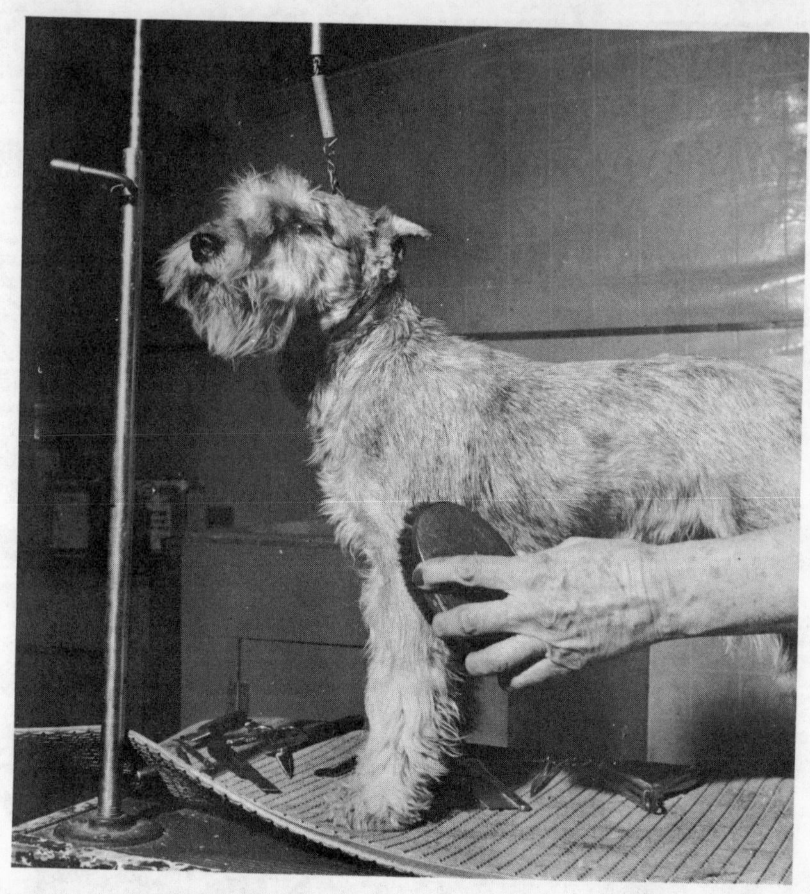

From the look on his face, this Schnauzer is enjoying his grooming. Brush the leg feathers thoroughly and use a soft brush for finishing touches.

and to stay there while you brush him, cut his nails, and give him a complete inspection.

Your dog will seldom need a bath, as Miniature Schnauzers have no body odor, but the leg furnishings and whiskers should be washed fairly often. This not only promotes a profuse growth, but removes any dirt left in the hair or food in the whiskers. Too much bathing will dry the skin and cause shedding, so don't overdo it in any event. If you use soap be sure to rinse it all out so that the residue won't irritate his skin. He should be dried off and kept in a warm place afterward, so he won't be chilled.

If your dog's skin is dry or if he sheds more than a little bit in spring and fall, it may be due to lack of fat in his diet. Rub a little olive oil into his

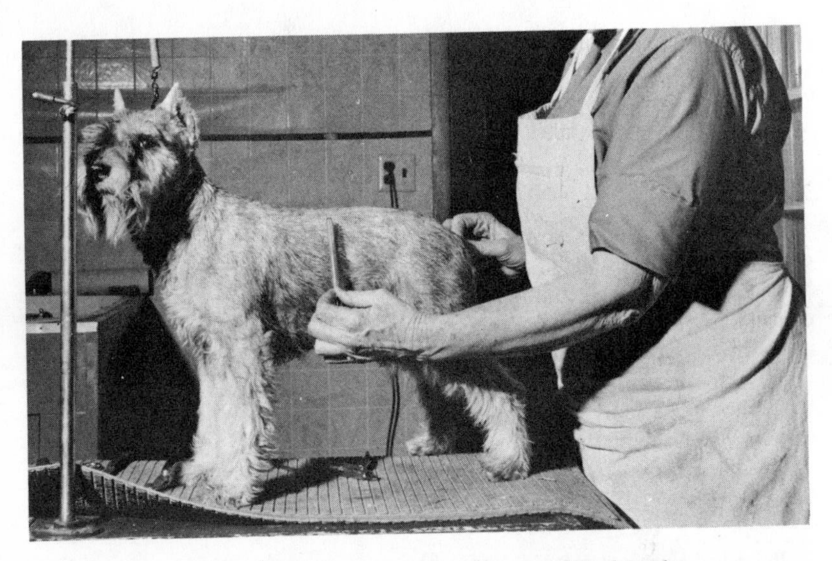

Above: Comb your Schnauzer to remove snarls and tangles.

Below: Teach your dog to stand quietly on a grooming table.

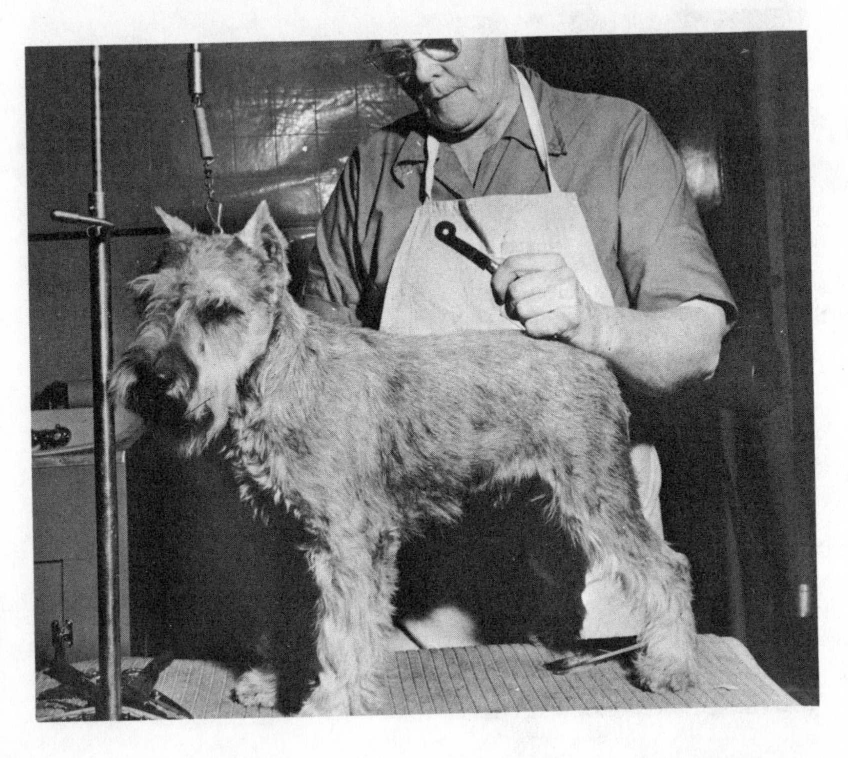

coat and add a spoonful of lard to his food. Other skin troubles, shown by scratching, redness, or a sore on the surface, should be examined by your veterinarian, who can prescribe treatment and clear up the trouble quickly. Don't delay, as once it takes hold any skin disease is hard to cure.

NOSE, TEETH, EARS AND EYES

Normally, a dog's nose, teeth, ears and eyes need no special care. The dog's nose is cool and moist to the touch (unless he has been in a warm house); however, the "cold nose" theory is only a partial indication of health or sickness. A fever, for instance, would be shown by a hot, dry nose, but other illness might not cause this. The dog's eyes are normally bright and alert, with the eyelid down in the corner, not over the eye. If the haw is bloodshot or partially covers the eye, it may be a sign of illness or irritation. If your dog has matter in the corners of the eyes, bathe with a mild eye wash; obtain ointment from your veterinarian or pet shop to treat a chronic condition.

The veterinarian will use a dentist's tool to remove tartar from your Schnauzer's teeth. With a well-balanced diet and a hard bone, your dog's teeth will remain in good condition.

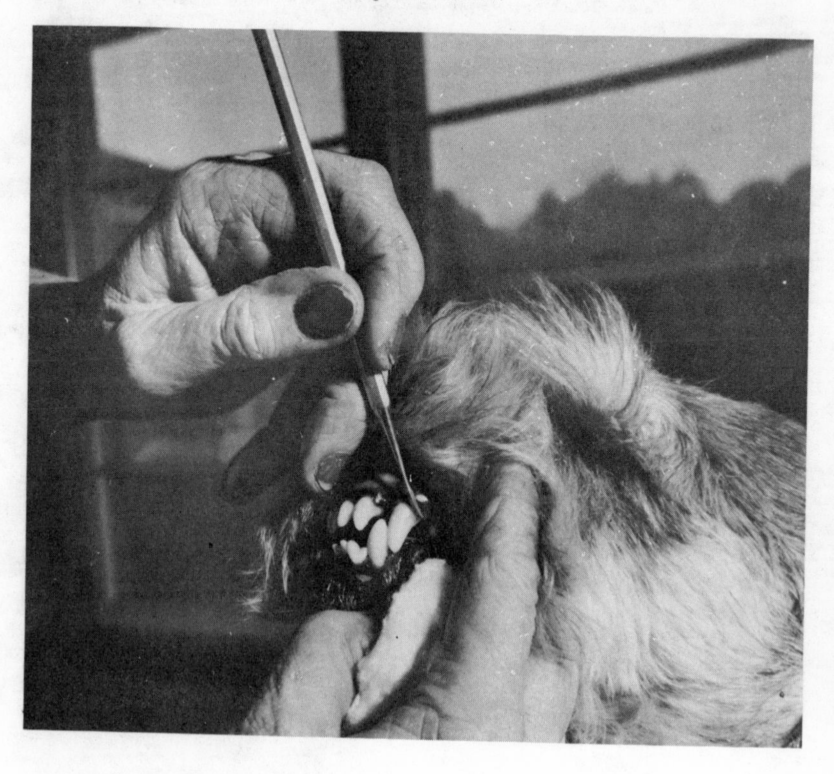

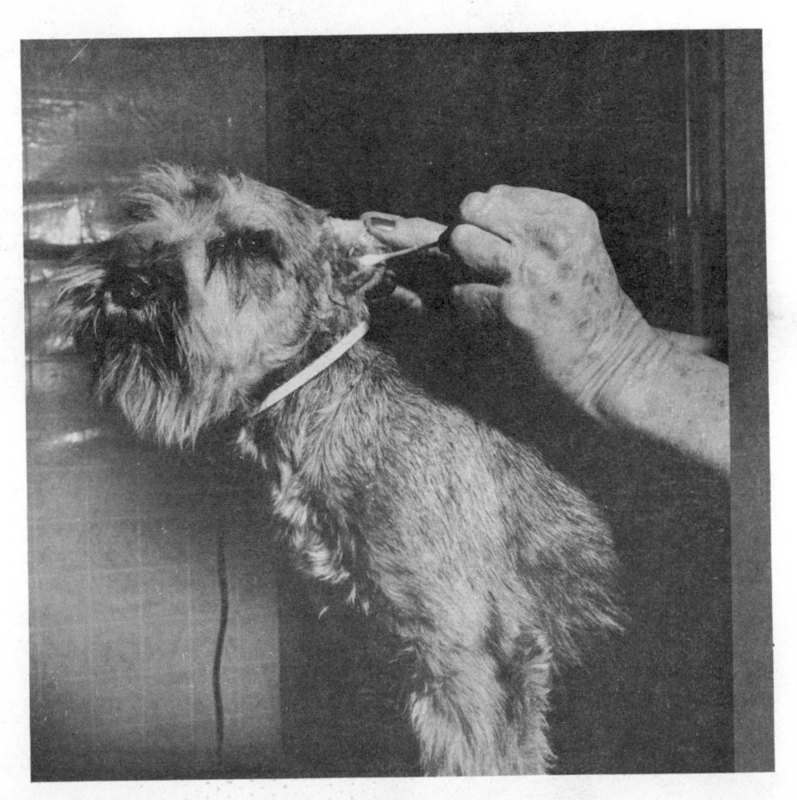

Be very careful when you examine or treat your dog's ears.

If your dog seems to have something wrong with his ears which causes him to scratch them or shake his head, cautiously probe the ear with a cotton swab. An accumulation of wax will probably work itself out. But dirt or dried blood is indicative of ear mites or infection, and should be treated immediately. Sore ears in the summer, due to fly bites, should be washed with mild soap and water, then covered with a soothing ointment, gauze-wrapped if necessary. Keep the dog protected from insects, and if necessary keep him indoors until his ears heal.

The dog's teeth will take care of themselves, although you may want your veterinarian to scrape off the unsightly tartar accumulation occasionally. A good hard bone will help to do the same thing.

TOENAILS

Keep your dog's toenails short with a weekly clipping. Use specially designed clippers that are available at your pet shop. Never take off too much at one time, as you might cut the "quick" which is sensitive and will bleed. Cut the nails straight across, then round off the sides with a little clip or a file. Be particularly careful when you cut black nails in which the quick is not visible.

PARASITES

If your dog picks up fleas or other skin parasites from neighbors' dogs or from the ground, weekly use of a good DDT- or Chlordane-base flea powder will get rid of them. Remember to dust his bed and change the bedding, too, as flea eggs drop off the host to hatch and wait in likely places for the dog to return. In warm weather a weekly dusting or monthly dip is good prevention.

If your grown dog is well-fed and in good health you will probably have no trouble with worms. He may pick them up from other dogs, however, so if you suspect worms, have a stool examination made and, if necessary, worm him. Fleas, too, are carriers of tapeworm, so that is one good reason to make sure the dog is free from these insects. Roundworms, the dog's most common intestinal parasite, have a life cycle which permits

When you have to give your Miniature Schnauzer a pill, hold him firmly, push it as far as possible down his throat and hold his mouth closed until he swallows.

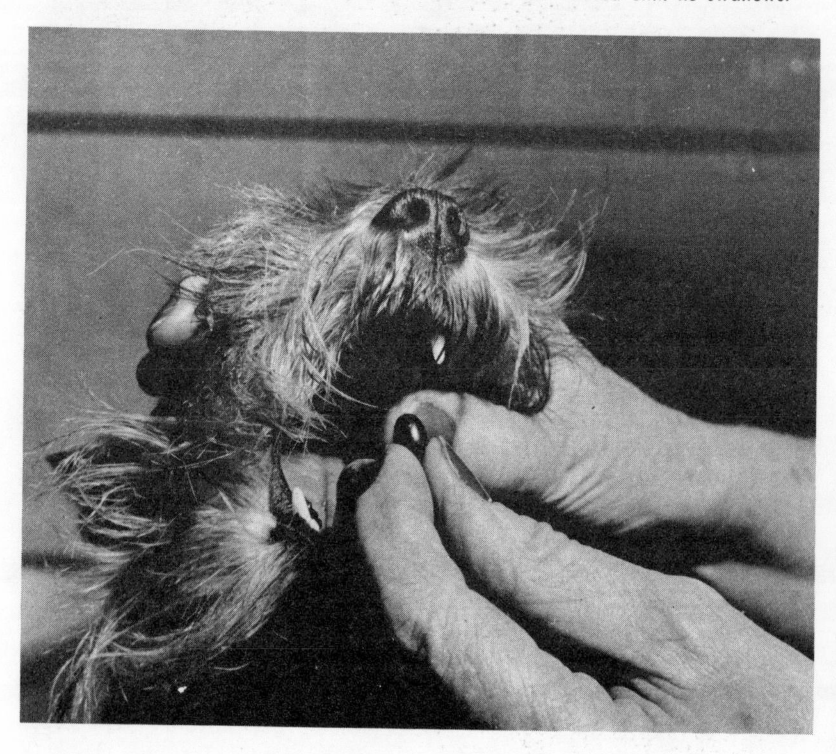

Above: Before you trim your Schnauzer's nails, push back the hair between his toes or, better still, cut it short.

Below: If you are firm and gentle with your dog, he will not mind having his nails clipped.

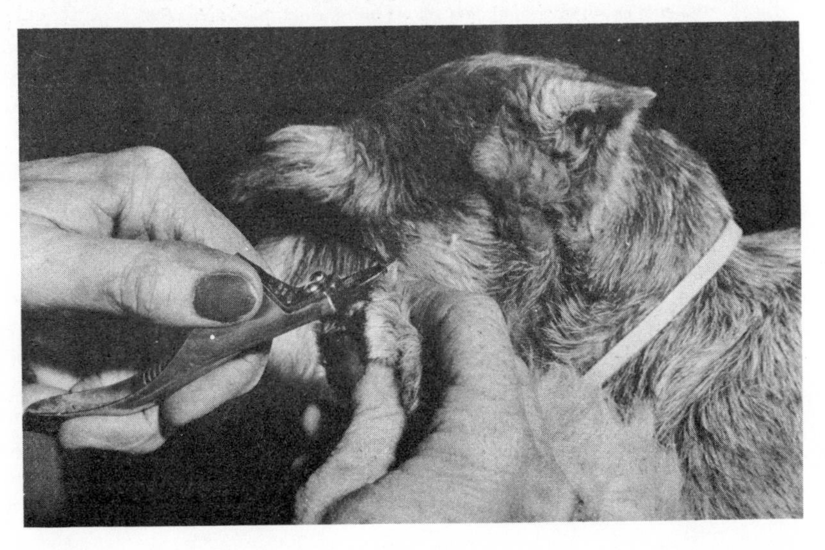

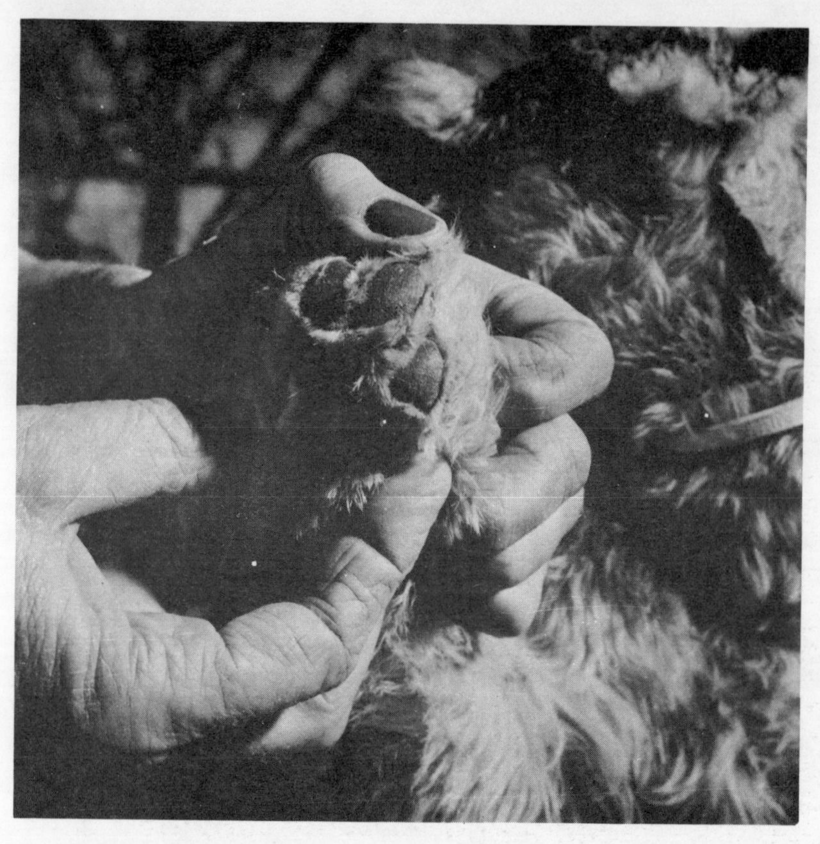

The long hair between the toes should be cut short for neat, healthy feet.

complete eradication by worming twice, ten days apart. The first worming will remove all adults and the second will destroy all subsequently hatched eggs before they in turn can produce more parasites.

FIRST AID

If your dog is injured, you can give him first aid which is, in general, similar to that for a human. The same principles apply. Superficial wounds should be disinfected and healing ointment applied. If the cut is likely to get dirty apply a bandage and restrain the dog so that he won't keep trying to remove it. A cardboard ruff will prevent him from licking his chest or body. Nails can be taped down to prevent scratching.

A board splint should be put on before moving a dog that might have a broken bone. If you are afraid that the dog will bite from pain, use a bandage muzzle made from a long strip of cloth, wrapped around the muzzle, then tied under the jaw and brought up behind the ears to hold it

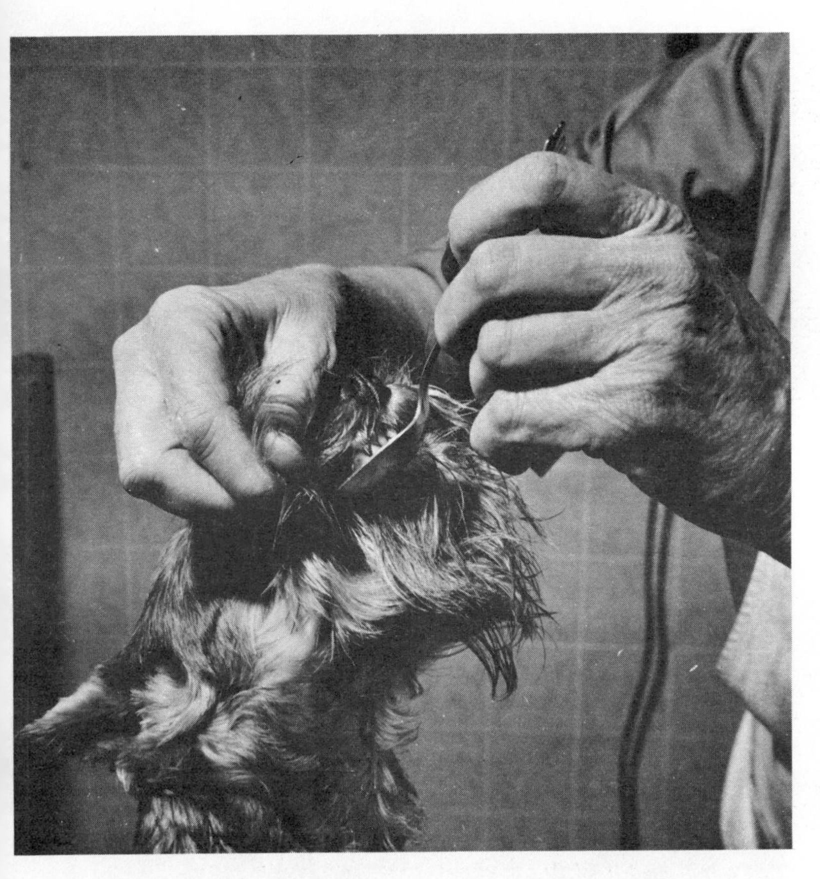

When you have to give your dog liquid medicine, pour it into his mouth and hold his head up until he swallows it, so he doesn't choke or spit it out.

on. In case of severe bleeding on a limb, apply a tourniquet—a strip of cloth wrapped around a stick to tighten it will do—between the cut and the heart, but loosen it every few minutes to avoid damaging the circulation.

If you suspect that your dog has swallowed poison, try to get him to vomit by giving him salt water or mustard in water. In all these cases, rush him to your veterinarian as soon as possible, after alerting the vet by phone.

In warm weather the most important thing to remember for your dog's sake is providing fresh water. If he tends to slobber and drink too much, it may be offered at intervals of an hour or so instead of being available at all times, but it should be fresh and cool. Don't overexercise the dog or let the children play too wildly with him in the heat of the day. Don't leave him outside without shade, and never leave a dog in a car which would become overheated in the sun. It should always have some shade and ventilation through the windows.

THE OLD DOG

With the increased knowledge and care available, there is no reas why your dog should not live to a good old age. As he grows older he ma need a little additional care, however. Remember that a fat dog is not health particularly as he grows older, and limit his food accordingly. The old dog needs exercise as much as ever, although his heart cannot bear th strain of sudden and violent exertion. His digestion may not be as good it was as a puppy, so follow your veterinarian's advice about special feedin if necessary. Failing eyesight or hearing mean lessened awareness of danger so you must protect him more than before. The old dog is used to his hom and to set ways, so too many strangers are bound to be a strain. For th same reason, boarding him out or a trip to the vet's are to be avoided unle absolutely necessary.

Should you decide at this time to get a puppy, to avoid being witho a dog when your old retainer is no longer with you, be very careful ho you introduce the puppy. He is naturally playful and will expect the old dog to respond to his advances. Sometimes the old dog will get a new lea on life from a pup. But don't make him jealous by giving to the newcom the attention that formerly was exclusively his. Feed them apart, and sho the old dog that you still love him the most; the puppy, not being used t individual attention, will not mind sharing your love.

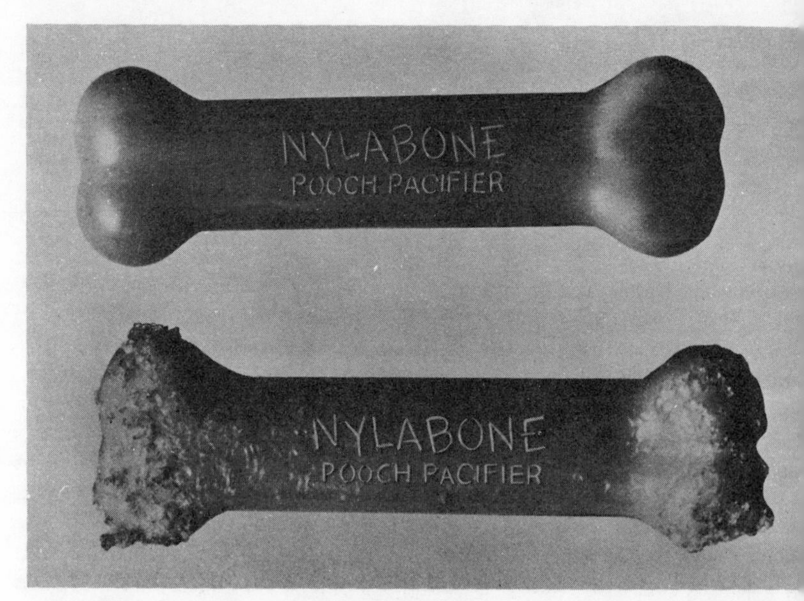

NYLABONE® is a necessity that is available at your local petshop (not in supermarkets). T puppy or grown dog chews the hambone flavored nylon into a frilly dog toothbrush, ma saging his gums and cleaning his teeth as he plays. Veterinarians highly recommend th product . . . but beware of cheap imitations which might splinter or break.

. How to Train Your Miniature Schnauzer

The Miniature Schnauzer can be easily trained to become a well-behaved mber of your family. Training should begin the day you get him. Although uppy under six months is too young for you to expect much in the way of edience, you should teach him to respect your authority. Be consistent. Don't ow the pup to jump all over you when you are wearing old clothes, because u can't expect him to know the difference when you are dressed for a party. n't encourage the dog to climb into your lap or onto your bed, then nish him for leaving mud on furniture when you aren't around. Although months to a year is the best time to begin serious training, a dog of any e can learn if you use consideration and patience. You *can* teach an d dog new tricks.

Housebreaking has already been covered. You cannot expect perfection om a puppy, or even an older dog, particularly if he is not used to living a house. A dog in a strange place is likely to be ill at ease and make a istake for that reason. Remember that once this has happened, you can nly prevent further accidents by not allowing the opportunity to arise. Be re to remove all traces which would remind the dog of previous errors.

A young puppy must relieve himself frequently, so do not let him roam roughout the house and don't shut him up without papers or a box if you ish to keep him from using the floor or rug. If you are careless you will so let a puppy get into the habit of chewing things up or being otherwise ischievous; he should not be left where he can get into trouble.

After you have taught your dog to be clean indoors and to relieve imself outside, you should teach him to do it on command, not only in one amiliar place. It is a convenience when traveling to be able to keep him n leash, so take the time to teach him before it is necessary. "Curb your og" is the rule in most cities; for the sake of others you should teach your og to obey it.

This excellent specimen of a Miniature Schnauzer has been trained to stand correctly. Here he demonstrates the correct show pose.

GIVING COMMANDS

When you give commands use the shortest phrase possible and use th same word with the same meaning at all times. If you want to teach your do to sit, then always use the word SIT. If you want your dog to lie down, the always use the word DOWN. It doesn't matter what word you use as lon as your dog becomes accustomed to hearing it and acts upon it.

The trick dog that always sits on the command UP and stands at SIT was trained to obey the words that way, since words are merely sound to him. Your dog does not understand what you say, but associates the wor with his training and the tone of your voice. Unless you use command consistently your dog will never learn to obey promptly.

LESSONS

Try to make your training lessons interesting. Short, frequent lesson are of much more value than long ones occasionally. It is better to trai your dog 10 minutes a day than 30 minutes once a week.

The most important part of all training is the reward—it is even more ɔortant than punishment. Give your dog plenty of praise and affection en he behaves. An occasional dog biscuit treat is all right, but do not bribe ır dog to obey, as he will come to depend on the crutch instead of obeying the sake of his love for you. Training him will bring you closer together l make a happier dog and owner.

ƆLLAR AND LEASH

Your puppy should become used to a leash and collar at an early age. If is ever allowed off your property, or if he might accidentally stray, he ɔuld have an identification tag attached to his collar and wear it at all ıes, although he does not usually need to be licensed until he is six months l. Check with local authorities on regulations. A leather collar will be out-ɔwn several times before your dog is full-grown, so buy a lightweight collar at fits him well and choose it for use, not for fancy looks. The leash should o be leather or cord, with a strong swivel clip on one end. Do not use a ain – it is heavy and may frighten the puppy, and it is painful if he should ngle you up as he is learning to walk properly. A choke collar for training usually made of chrome chain, and for your small Schnauzer you will ant the lightest weight watch chain. Never leave a choke collar on a dog large, as it could catch on his hair or on a twig and choke him. It is useful r training because it pulls and releases as you do, and exerts more direct essure than an ordinary collar.

Let the puppy wear his collar around until he is used to its feel and eight. After several short periods he will not be distracted by the strange-ess and you can attach the leash. Let him pull it around and then try to ad him a bit. He will probably resist, bucking and balking, or simply sitting own and refusing to budge. Fight him for a few minutes, dragging him along necessary, but then let him relax for the day, with plenty of affection nd praise. He won't be lead-broken until he learns that he must obey the ull under any circumstance, but don't try to do it in one lesson. Ten ninutes a day is long enough for any training. The dog's period of concen-tration is short and, like a child, he will become bored if you carry it on ɔo long.

IEELING

Once the puppy obeys the pull of the leash half your training is accom-plished. "Heeling" is a necessity for a well-behaved dog, so teach him to valk at your left side, head up and even with your knee. It is annoying to passers-by and other dog-owners to have a dog, however friendly, bear down n them and entangle dogs, people and packages.

To teach your dog, start off walking briskly, saying "Heel" in a firm voice. Pull back with a sharp jerk if he lunges ahead, and if he lags repeat the command and tug on the leash, not allowing him to drag behind. After

Teach your dog to stand still, and place his feet in the correct position for showing.

the dog has learned to heel at various speeds on leash, you can remove and practice heeling free, but have it ready to snap on again as soon as wanders. With all parts of the training, go back to the step before if the d does not improve, and start each new step in a quiet place free fro distractions.

You must understand that most dogs like to stop and sniff around a b until they find *the* place to do their duty. Be kind enough to stop and wa for your dog when he finds it necessary to pause.

TEACHING YOUR DOG TO COME, SIT, STAY AND LIE DOWN

When the dog understands the pull of the leash he should learn come. Never call him to you for punishment, or he will be quick to disobey th mmand. Always go to him if he has been disobedient. To teach him to come, him reach the end of a long lead, then give the command, pulling him vard you at the same time. As soon as he associates the word "Come" with action, pull only when he does not respond immediately. As he starts come, back up to make him learn that he must come from a distance as ll as when he is close to you. Soon you can practice without a leash, but he is slow to come or actively disobedient, go to him and pull him toward u, repeating the command. More practice with leash on is needed.

"Sit," "Down," and "Stay" are among the most useful commands and ll make it easier for you to control your dog on many occasions—during ooming, veterinary care, walks when you meet a strange dog, drives in

With his head and tail up, this Miniature Schnauzer is the picture of alertness. He shows the typical terrier expression as he looks at the camera.

the car, and so forth. Teaching him to sit is the first step. With collar a leash on have him stand in the "Heel" position. Give the command "Si at the same time pulling up on the leash in your right hand and pressi down on his hindquarters with your left. As soon as he sits, release t pressure and praise him. After a few times, push him down again if he ris immediately, and then make him sit with voice command only, and fro varying positions.

To teach your dog to stay, bring your hand close to his face with direct motion at the same time as you give the order. Ask him to rema only a few seconds at first, but gradually the time can be increased and y

This young show prospect is being trained to pose for the judge, but training your dog to sit, lie down and be generally well-behaved requires equal patience and firmness.

A wire run like this is an excellent place for puppies to get sun and exercise. Grown dogs should have a permanent fence supported by posts, with a dog house or some protection from the weather.

can leave him at a distance. If he should move, return immediately and make him sit and stay again, after you scold him.

To teach your dog to lie down, have him sit facing you. Pull down on the leash by putting your foot on it and pulling at the same time as you say "Down." Gesture toward the ground with a sweep of your arm. When he begins to understand what is wanted, do it without the leash and alternate voice and hand signals. Teach him to lie down from standing as well as sitting position, and begin to do it from a distance. Hand signals are particularly useful when your dog can see you but is too far away to hear, and they may be used in teaching all commands.

DISCIPLINE TRAINING

If you are consistent in your training and stop the puppy every time he starts to misbehave, he is not likely to get into bad habits. Every puppy goes through a teething period, but if he has his own toy or bone he won't chew up the furniture. If the puppy learns not to jump up, and to stay off the furniture, he will not pick up the habit later on. If you call him back to you or jerk his leash when he wants to chase a car or bicycle, he will soon learn that it is forbidden. Excessive barking can soon be cured by a scolding, or, if necessary, by spanking lightly with a folded newspaper or dousing with a glass of water. Your dog must be disciplined every time he misbehaves; haphazard training will only confuse him.

With a dog that has already acquired bad habits, stronger measures are needed. If he jumps on people, knock him off balance with a well-aimed knee, or step on his hind toes, *at the same time as you say "no."* You can cure him of chasing cars with a water pistol or a whole bucket of water dumped on his unsuspecting head. If you catch him in the act from behind you will also spoil his fun.

Prevention of all bad habits is easier than cure, and there is no reason why you cannot train your dog. There are many books on the subject in your local public library, and many towns have obedience training classes which hold weekly meetings with an experienced trainer to help you teach your dog. We strongly recommend taking your dog to class; the A.K.C. or Gaines Dog Research Center can supply a list of near-by classes.

TRICKS

Most dogs learn a few tricks without even trying. With patient training you can teach your dog to shake paws, roll over, sit up, beg, and do many other tricks.

To teach your Schnauzer to shake hands, first have him sit. Then, upon the command "Paw," lift his paw in your hand and shake it vigorously without knocking him off balance. Then give him lots of praise. Repeat this several times a day and in a week he will all but hold out his paw when you walk in the door!

Teach him to beg in the same way. Have him sit, and, as you give the command "Beg," lift his front paws up until he is in a begging position. Hold him that way until he finds a comfortable balance; then let him balance himself, and hold a piece of dog candy over his nose. Release his paws, lower the candy to his mouth, and hold it firmly so he has to pry it loose. Repeat the command "Beg" over and over until he assumes the position upon the command. Reward him whenever he obeys.

If you wish to teach your Schnauzer to sit up or beg, lift him up as you give the command, and reward him each time until he catches on. Always be generous with your praise.

6. Caring for the Female and Raising Puppies

Whether or not you bought your female dog intending to breed her, some preparation is necessary when and if you decide to take this step.

WHEN TO BREED

It is usually best to breed on the second or third season. Plan in advance the time of year which is best for you, taking into account where the puppies will be born and raised. You will keep them until they are at least six weeks old, and a litter of husky pups takes up considerable space by then. Other considerations are selling the puppies (Christmas vs. springtime sales), your own vacation, and time available to care for them. You'll need at least an hour a day to feed and clean up after the mother and puppies but probably it will take you much longer – with time out to admire and play with them!

CHOOSING THE STUD

You can plan to breed your female about 6½ months after the start of her last season, although a variation of a month or two either way is not unusual. Choose the stud dog and make arrangements well in advance. If you are breeding for show stock, which may command better prices, a mate should be chosen with an eye to complementing the deficiencies of your female. If possible, the dogs should have several ancestors in common within the last two or three generations, as such combinations generally "click" best. The male should have a good show record or be the sire of show winners if old enough to be proven.

The owner of such a male usually charges a fee for the use of the dog. This does not guarantee a litter, but you generally have the right to breed your female again if she does not have puppies. In some cases the owner of the stud will agree to take a choice puppy in place of a stud fee. You should settle all details beforehand, including the possibility of a single surviving puppy, deciding the age at which he is to make his choice and take the pup, and so on.

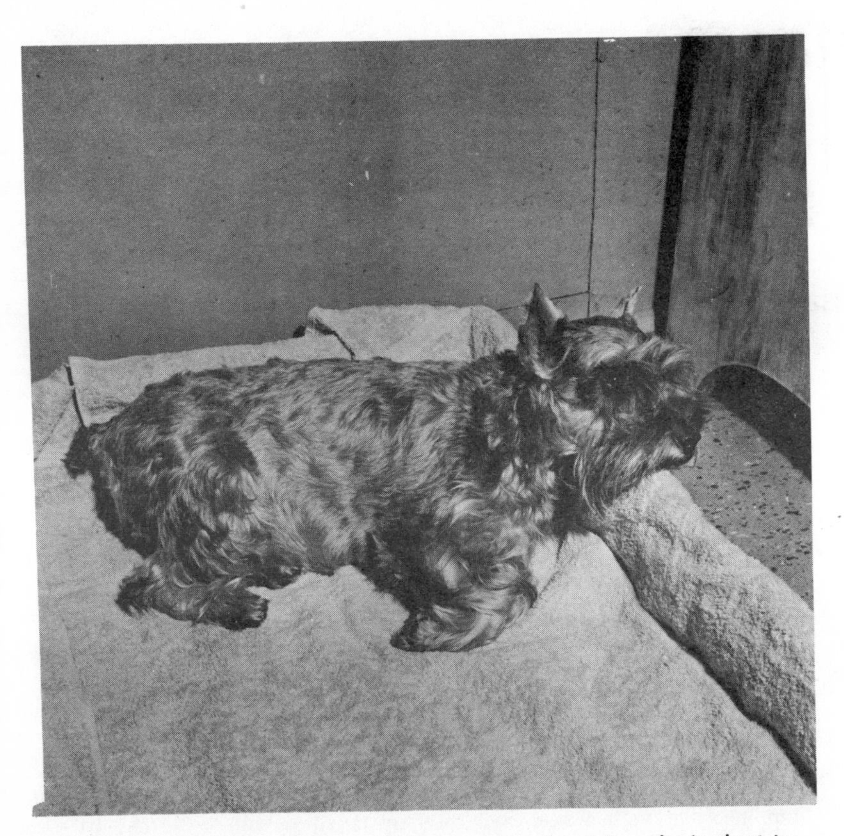

Provide a whelping box in an out-of-the-way corner for a dog who is about to become a mother. Line the box with newspapers, an old quilt or blanket.

If you want to raise a litter "just for the fun of it" and plan merely to make use of an available male, the most important selection point is temperament. Make sure the dog is friendly as well as healthy, because a bad disposition could appear in his puppies, and this is the worst of all traits in a dog destined to be a pet. In such cases a "stud fee puppy," not necessarily the choice of the litter, is the usual payment.

PREPARATION FOR BREEDING

Before you breed your female, make sure she is in good health. She should be neither too thin nor too fat. Any skin disease *must* be cured before it can be passed on to the puppies. If she has worms she should be wormed before being bred or within three weeks afterward. It is generally considered a good idea to revaccinate her against distemper and hepatitis before the puppies are born. This will increase the immunity the puppies receive during their early, most vulnerable period.

The female will probably be ready to breed 12 days after the first colored discharge. You can usually make arrangements to board her with the owner of the male for a few days, to insure her being there at the proper time, or you can take her to be mated and bring her home the same day. If she still appears receptive she may be bred again two days later. However, some females never show signs of willingness, so it helps to have the experience of a breeder. Usually the second day after the discharge changes color is the proper time, and she may be bred for about three days following. For an additional week or so she may have some discharge and attract other dogs by her odor, but can seldom be bred.

THE FEMALE IN WHELP

You can expect the puppies nine weeks from the day of breeding, although 61 days is as common as 63. During this time the female should receive normal care and exercise. If she was overweight, don't increase her food at first; excess weight at whelping time is bad. If she is on the thin side build her up, giving some milk and biscuit at noon if she likes it. You may add one of the mineral and vitamin supplements to her food to make sure that the puppies will be healthy. As her appetite increases, feed her more. During the last two weeks the puppies grow enormously and she will probably have little room for food and less appetite. She should be tempted with meat, liver and milk, however. Divide her meals into three or four feedings per day, since she will no longer have room for all the food she needs at one time.

As the female in whelp grows heavier, cut out violent exercise and jumping. Although a dog used to such activities will often play with the children or run around voluntarily, restrain her for her own sake.

PREPARING FOR THE PUPPIES

Prepare a whelping box a few days before the puppies are due, and allow the mother to sleep there overnight or to spend some time in it during the day to become accustomed to it. Then she is less likely to try to have her pups under the front porch or in the middle of your bed. A variety of places will serve, such as a corner of your cellar, garage, or an unused room. A whelping box serves to separate mother and puppies from visitors and other distractions. The walls should be high enough to restrain the puppies, yet allow the mother to get away from the puppies after she has fed them. Three feet square is minimum size, and eight-inch walls will keep the pups in until they begin to climb, when the walls should be built up. Then the puppies really need more room anyway, so double the space with a very low partition down the middle and you will find them naturally housebreaking themselves.

Layers of newspaper spread over the whole area will make excellent bedding and be absorbent enough to keep the surface warm and dry. They

This litter of husky Schnauzer puppies enjoy dinner while their mother poses proudly for the photographer. When the puppies fall asleep the mother can leave the box for a while. She is much better off than if she were penned up with the puppies in too small a space.

should be removed daily and replaced with another thick layer. An old quilt or washable blanket makes better footing for the nursing puppies than slippery newspaper during the first week, and is softer for the mother.

Be prepared for the actual whelping several days in advance. Usually the female will tear up papers, refuse food and generally act restless. These may be false alarms; the real test is her temperature, which will drop to below 100° about 12 hours before whelping. Take it with a rectal thermometer morning and evening, and when the temperature goes down put her in the pen, looking in on her frequently.

WHELPING

Usually little help is needed but it is wise to stay close to make sure that the mother's lack of experience does not cause an unnecessary accident. Be ready to help when the first puppy arrives, for it could smother if the mother does not break the membrane enclosing it. She should start right away to lick the puppy, drying and stimulating it, but you can do it with a soft rough towel instead. The afterbirth should follow the birth of each puppy, attached to the puppy by the long umbilical cord. Watch to make sure that each is expelled, for retaining this material can cause infection. In her instinct for cleanliness the mother will probably eat the afterbirth after biting the cord. One or two will not hurt her; they stimulate milk supply as well as labor for remaining pups. But too many can make her lose appetite for the food she needs to feed her pups and regain her strength. So remove the rest of them along with the wet newspapers and keep the pen dry and clean to relieve her anxiety.

If the mother does not bite the cord, or does it too close to the body, take over the job, to prevent an umbilical hernia. Tearing is recommended, but you can cut it, about two inches from the body, with a sawing motion of scissors that have been sterilized in alcohol. Then dip the end of the cord in a shallow dish of iodine; the cord will dry up and fall off in a few days.

The puppies should follow each other at intervals of not more than half an hour. If more time goes past and you are sure there are still pups to come, a brisk walk outside may start labor again. If your dog is actively straining without producing a puppy it may be presented backward, a so-called "breech" or upside-down birth. Careful assistance with a well-soaped finger to feel for the puppy or ease it back may help, but never attempt to pull it by force against the mother. This could cause serious damage, so let an expert handle it.

If anything seems wrong, waste no time in calling your veterinarian who can examine her and if necessary give hormones which will bring the remaining puppies. You may want his experience in whelping the litter even if all goes well. He will probably prefer to have the puppies born at his hospital rather than to get up in the middle of the night to come to your home. The mother would, no doubt, prefer to stay at home, but you can be sure she will get the best of care in his hospital. If the puppies are born at home and all goes as it should, watch the mother carefully afterward. It is wise to have the veterinarian check her and the pups, anyway, and you will want to have tails docked and dewclaws removed at two to four days. This is definitely no job for an amateur, so leave it to the expert.

RAISING THE PUPPIES

Hold each puppy to a breast as soon as he is dry, for a good meal without competition. Then he may join his littermates in a basket out of his mother's way while she is whelping. Keep a supply of evaporated milk on hand for emergencies, or later weaning. A formula of evaporated milk, corn syrup and a little water with egg yolk should be warmed and fed in a doll or baby bottle if necessary. A supplementary feeding often helps weak pups over the hump. Keep track of birth weights, and take weekly readings thereafter for an accurate record of the pups' growth and health.

After the puppies have arrived, take the mother outside for a walk and drink, and then leave her to take care of them. She will probably not want

When the puppy is two to four days old, the vet will dock his tail to the correct length. It is a simple operation when performed by an expert, and over so quickly the puppy will hardly know what has happened.

to stay away more than a minute or two for the first few weeks. Be sure to keep water available at all times, and feed her milk or broth frequently, as she needs liquids to produce milk. Encourage her to eat by giving her her favorite foods, until she asks for food of her own accord. She will soon develop a ravenous appetite and should have at least two large meals a day, with dry food available in addition.

Prepare a warm place to put the puppies to keep them dry and help them to a good start in life. You can use a cardboard box in which you put an electric heating pad or hot water bottle covered with flannel. Set the box near the mother so that she can see her puppies. She will usually allow you

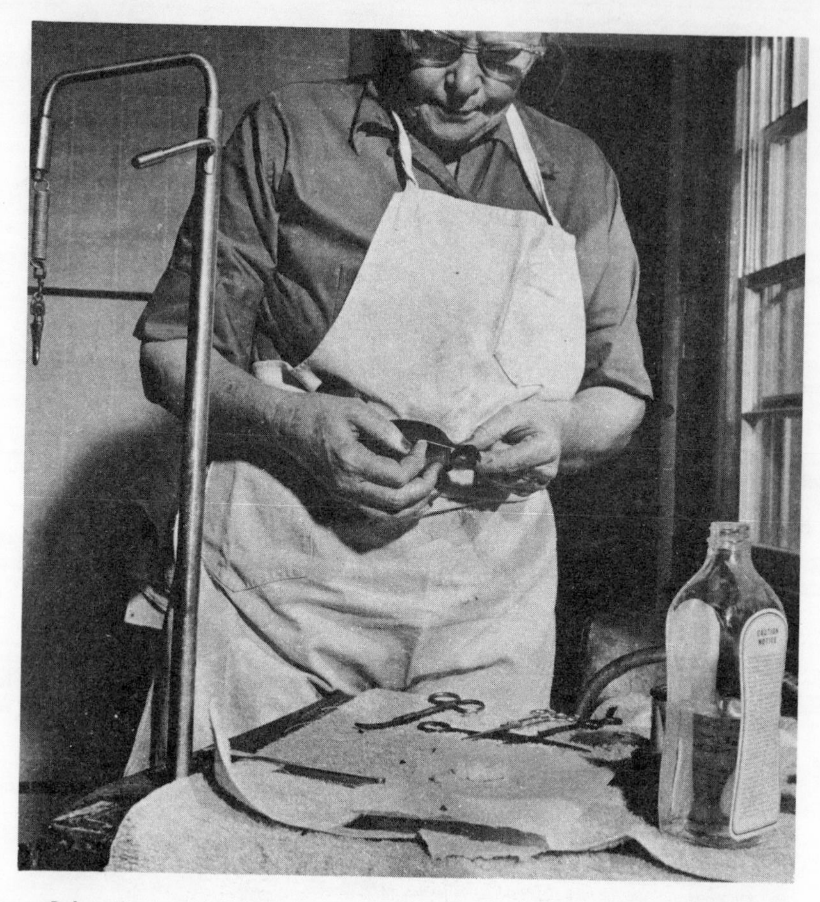

Before the puppy's tail is docked, a thread is tied around it, and afterward it is drawn tight to bring the skin together over the stump. The tail will heal in a few days.

to help, but don't take the puppies out of sight. Let her handle things if your interference seems to make her nervous.

Be sure that all the puppies are getting enough to eat. If the mother sits or stands instead of lying still to nurse, the probable cause is scratching from the puppies' nails. You can remedy this by clipping them, as you do hers. Manicure scissors will do for these tiny claws.

Some breeders advise disposing of the smaller or weaker pups in a large litter, since the mother has trouble in handling more than six or seven. But you can help her out by preparing an extra puppy box or basket. Leave half the litter with the mother and the other half in a warm place, changing off at two-hour intervals at first. Later you may change the pups less frequently, leaving them all together except during the day. Try supplementary feeding, too; as soon as their eyes open, at about two weeks, they will lap from a dish, anyway.

WEANING THE PUPPIES

The puppies should normally be completely weaned at five weeks, although you start to feed them at three weeks. They will find it easier to lap semi-solid food than to drink milk at first, so mix baby cereal with whole or evaporated milk, warmed to body temperature, and offer it to the puppies in a saucer. Until they learn to lap, it is best to feed one or two at a time, because they are more likely to walk into it than to eat. Hold the saucer at chin level, and let them gather around, keeping paws out of the dish. A damp sponge afterward prevents most of the cereal from sticking to their skin if

For a neat appearance it is important to have the tail exactly the right length — just long enough to be seen over the dog's back when he is grown.

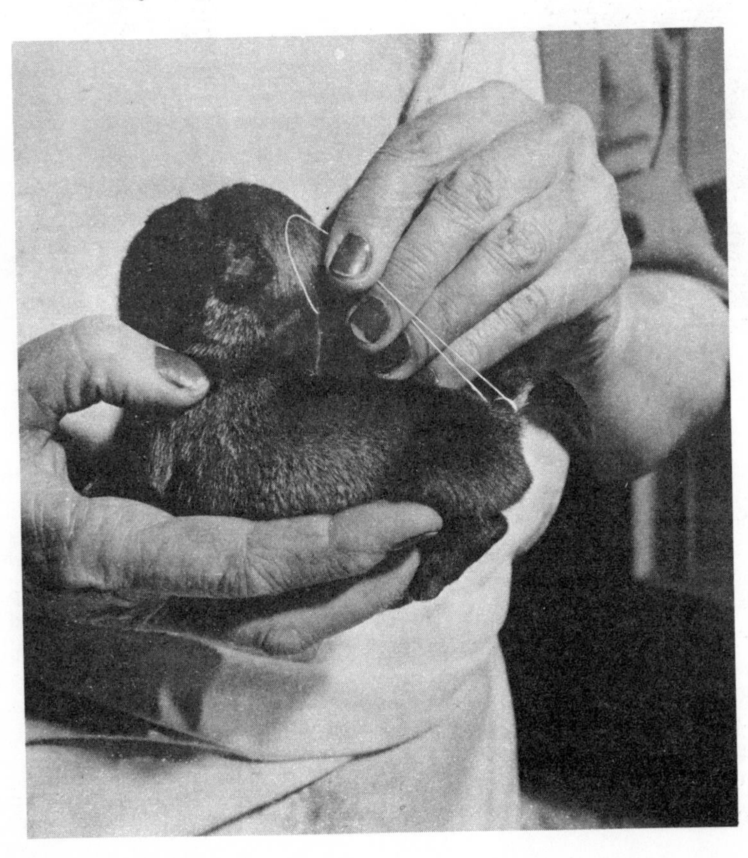

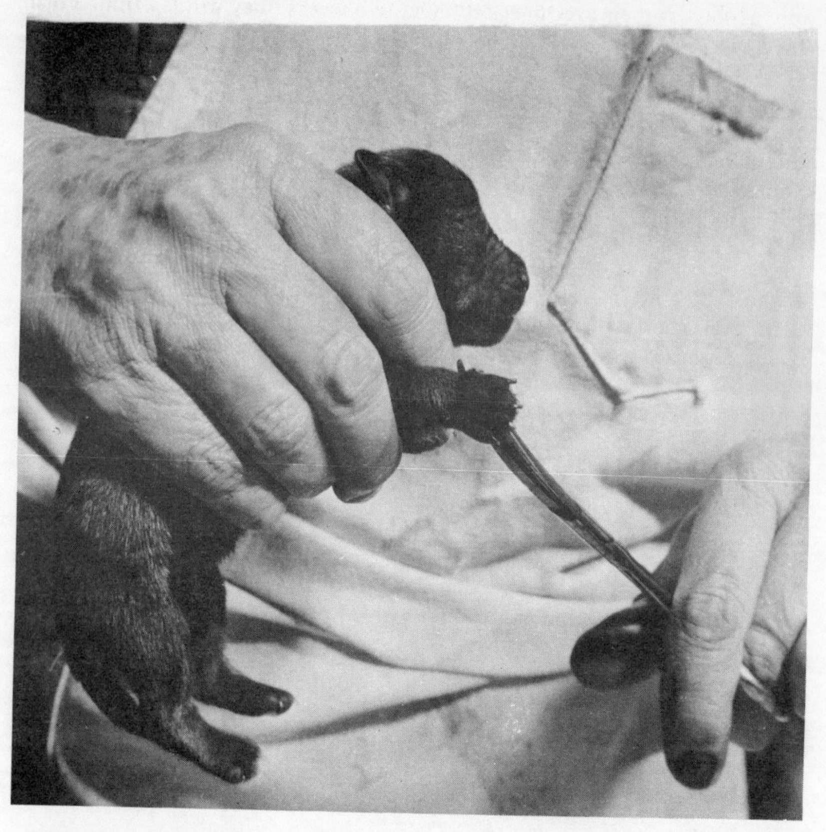

Have the vet remove the puppy's dewclaws at the same time the tail is docked.

the mother doesn't clean them up. Once they have gotten the idea, broth or babies' meat soup may be alternated with milk, and you can start them on finely chopped meat. At four weeks they will eat four meals a day, and soon do without their mother entirely. Don't leave water with them all the time; at this age everything is to play with and they will use it as a wading pool. They can drink all they need if it is offered several times a day, after meals.

As the puppies grow up the mother will go into the pen only to nurse them, first sitting up and then standing. To dry her up completely, keep her away from the puppies for longer periods; after a few days of part-time nursing she can stay away for still longer periods, and then completely. The little milk left will be resorbed.

The puppies may be put outside, unless it is too cold, as soon as their eyes are open, and will benefit from the sunlight and vitamins. Provide a box with a rubber mat or newspapers on the bottom to protect them from cold or damp. At six weeks they can go outside permanently unless it is very cold, but make sure that they go into their shelter at night or in bad weather. By now cleaning up is a man-sized job, so put them out at least during the day and make your task easier. Be sure to clean their run daily, as worms and other infections are lurking. You can expect the pups to need at least one worming before they are ready to go to new homes, so take a stool sample to your veterinarian before they are three weeks old. If one puppy has worms all should be wormed. Follow the veterinarian's advice, and this applies also to vaccination. If you plan to keep a pup you will want to vaccinate him at the earliest age, so his littermates should be done at the same time.

CROPPING YOUR PUPPIES' EARS

Your puppies' ears should be cropped at about nine weeks. First they should have the puppy fuzz stripped from their heads and necks. Be sure, whether or not anesthetic is given for the cropping, that the puppies are not fed before the operation is performed. Distract them if they want to scratch their ears afterward; if necessary, use a cardboard ruff to prevent scratching. Of course cropping is not required, even for the show ring, and it is not permitted in England, but an uncropped Schnauzer is rarely seen in this country. It is merely a matter of fashion.

Above: Cut a cardboard ruff like this one to prevent your puppy from scratching his ears after they are cropped.

Opposite page, above: Place the ruff around the puppy's neck and fasten it in position.

Opposite page, below: With his cropped ears taped down and his cardboard ruff on, this puppy looks sad, but his handsome appearance afterward will make it all worth while.

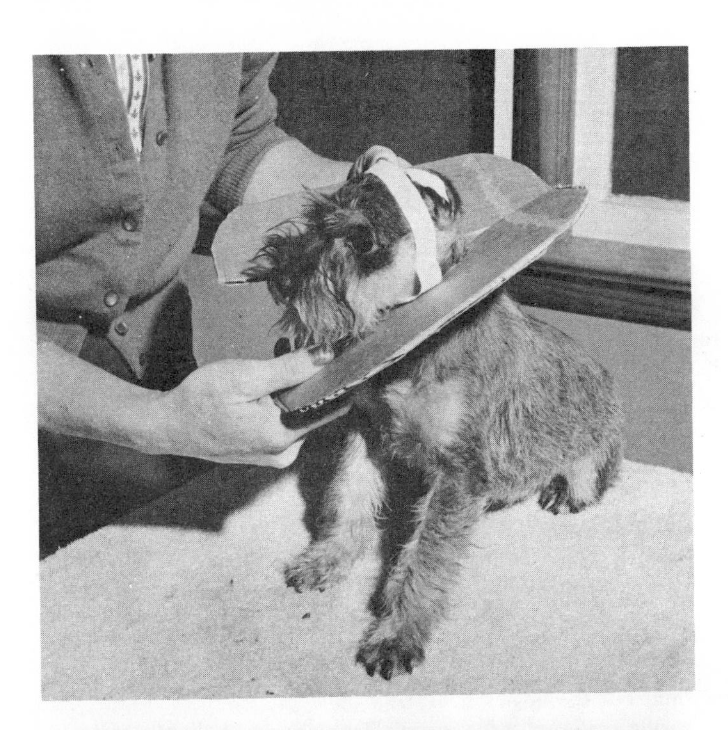

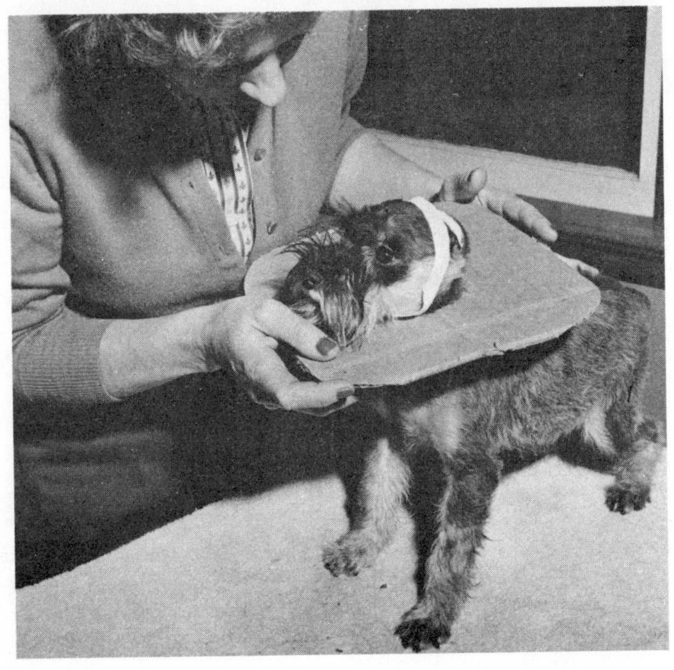

7. Showing Your Miniature Schnauzer

As your puppy grows he will doubtless have many admirers among your friends, some of whom are bound to say, "Oh, what a handsome dog —you should certainly show him!" Perhaps even a breeder or judge will say he has show possibilities, and although you didn't buy him with that thought in mind, "Cinderella" champions do come along now and then—often enough to keep dog breeders perennially optimistic.

If you do have ideas of showing your dog, get the opinion of someone with experience first. With favorable criticism, go ahead with your plans to show him. For the novice dog and handler, sanction shows are a good way to gain ring poise and experience. These are small shows often held by the local kennel club or breed specialty club. Entry fees are low and paid at the door, breeds and sexes are usually judged together, and the prizes and ribbons are not important. They provide a good opportunity to learn what goes on at a show, and to conquer ring nervousness. Matches are usually held during the evening or on a weekend afternoon, and you need stay only to be judged.

Before you go to a show your dog should be trained to gait at a trot beside you, with head up and in a straight line. In the ring you will have to gait around the edge with other dogs and then individually up and down the center runner. In addition the dog must stand for examination by the judge, who will look at him closely and feel his head and body structure. He should be taught to stand squarely, hind feet slightly back, head up on the alert. He must hold the pose when you place his feet and show animation for a piece of boiled liver in your hand or a toy mouse thrown in front of you.

ADVANCE PREPARATION

Showing requires practice training sessions in advance; get a friend to act as judge and set the dog up and "show" him for a few minutes every day.

Keep the dog's nails trimmed closely, for neat feet are important. His coat should also be kept in good condition, and it must be pulled by hand, not razored or sheared if the texture and color are not to be spoiled. A complete stripping must be done eight weeks in advance. Then daily attention

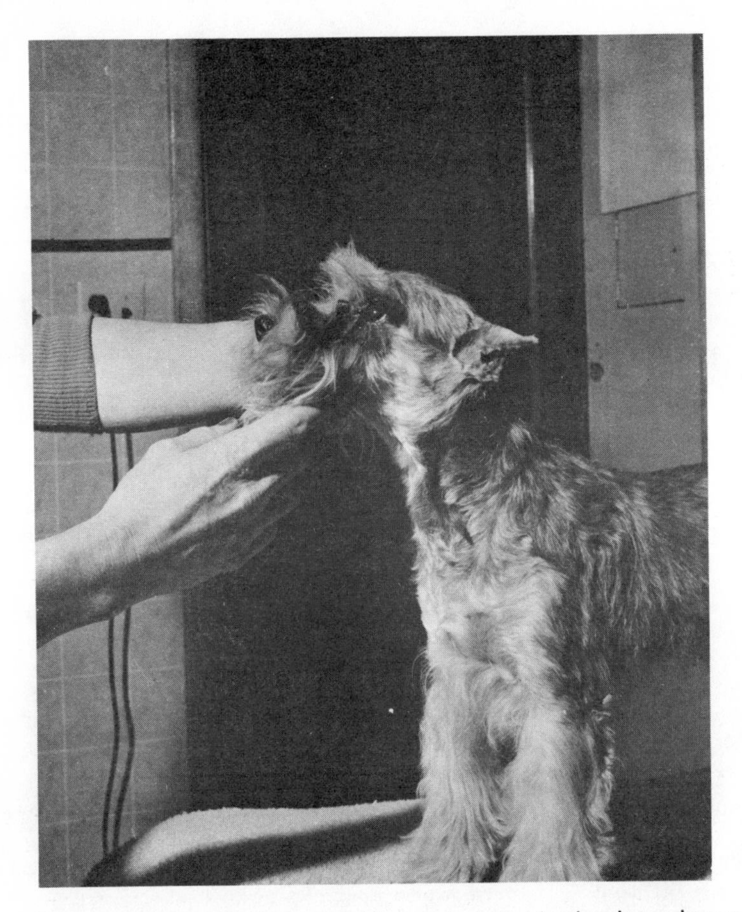

Before you show your Schnauzer, give him a last-minute trimming, but make sure you leave no rough edges. If you have given him a complete stripping well in advance, he will make a fine appearance in the show ring.

is necessary. The dog should be thoroughly brushed to remove loose hairs, and whiskers and furnishings must be kept scrupulously clean, free from mats and snarls. Do last-minute trimming the day before the show, but do not overdo it since rough edges will be glaringly obvious in the ring. The whiskers may have powdered chalk rubbed into them to whiten and give extra body, but be sure to brush it out thoroughly when it is dry. An extra polishing will make the hair lie flat where desired and stand out where you want it to. Stray hairs on the legs should be trimmed so that they have a smooth, even appearance all the way down.

To find out when dog shows will be held near you, write to the Gaines Dog Research Center, 250 Park Avenue, New York 17, N. Y., for a list of coming shows. Then write to the superintendent of the individual show for a premium list, and fill out the entry form as directed. You will probably want to go into the novice class (open to dogs that have not won a blue ribbon) or the puppy class if your Schnauzer is between six and twelve months old.

Pack your kit for the show the day before, putting in a water dish and some of the water the dog is used to, to prevent stomach upset (and to save you a trip to find water). A stout lead or bench chain should be used to fasten him to the bench if it is a benched show. You will also want your regular grooming equipment and a towel to keep him clean. The show lead is a light nylon or leather cord and collar in one piece, and shows off the dog to his best advantage.

Give your dog only a light meal the morning of the show; he will be more comfortable in the car and will show better in the ring. Be sure to arrive in plenty of time before the breed is to be judged. After you arrive and find where your dog is benched, with the other Miniature Schnauzers, give him a small drink and take him to the exercise ring to relieve himself. Give him a final grooming and be sure to be on time for your class.

THE SHOW

All male classes are first, in this order: puppy, novice, bred by exhibitor, American-bred, open. You can follow the judging with a catalogue purchased at the show, which gives owners, names and breeding of all entries.

The winners compete for Winners Dog, who is awarded points toward his championship according to the number present. The winner competes against the best female, then against champions entered in "specials only" for best of breed. The breed winner competes against other Terriers: Airedales, Scotties, Kerry Blues, Fox Terriers, and so forth, for best in this group, and the winner there goes on to try against Sporting, Hound, Working, Toy and Non-Sporting winners for the supreme award, Best in Show.

Another aspect of dog shows is the obedience trial. Any purebred dog may compete, to be judged on performance instead of conformation. There are three classes of increasing difficulty: novice, open and utility, leading to the degrees of C.D., C.D.X. and U.D.–companion dog (excellent) and utility dog.

If your dog has received the training we have described previously, he is well on the way to the necessary requirements for the novice class, and you may wish to continue. There are many obedience classes where an experienced trainer can help you with your dog; classes are held weekly at a nominal fee. It helps to accustom the dog to behaving in the company of others, but a daily training period at home is also necessary. For the novice class your dog must heel on and off leash, stand for examination, come when called, sit with you at the end of the ring for one minute, and lie down

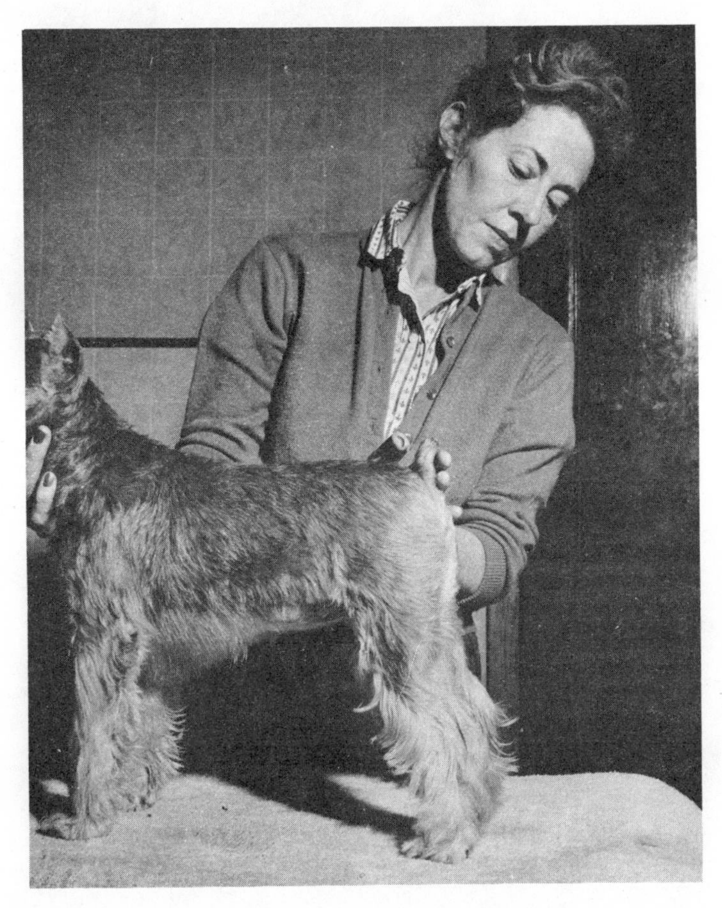

Ready for the show, this Miniature Schnauzer demonstrates the proper trimming of the body coat and hindquarters, with thick, wiry furnishings.

for three minutes. In advanced trials, retrieving, jumps, longer stays, and more difficult tasks are added. Attending an obedience class is excellent training for the show ring, or for a well-behaved dog you will be proud to own.